THE GREATEST

" How To Live Forever Series"

A Baby Boomer's Guide on "How To Live Forever Series" via Their Own Words and Ideas For Their Children and Grandchildren To Overcome Any Obstacle and Succeed

By James P Naughton

KEY
Publishing Company

The Greatest

ISBN 978-0-9858377-4-7

www.KeyPublishingCompany.com

LinkedIn

Facebook

Printed in the United States of America

Cover designed by Kip Williams

Author photo on cover by Alan Hubbard

Book editing, layout, and design by
Kip Williams Design®
mrkipw@gmail.com

Goals of the book:

My book is intended to do three things:

1. To give my Baby Boomer generation ideas on living forever along with four previous books and a newspaper article that I list at the end.

2. To provide their children and grandchildren and other young people who may be stuck or facing difficult challenges in their lives, with ideas and real-life examples that will enable them to be successful in business and life no matter how difficult their situation might seem and no matter what obstacles that they feel are blocking their path to success.

3. To provide entertainment using the author's real-life stories from the era, especially for those 76 million Baby Boomers who grew up in blue-collar factory towns across the country. And also share the stories with those who grew up in and around our great cities during the era.

I dedicate this book first to my wife, Sharon, my children, Matthew, Erin, Timothy, and my daughter-in-law Cristina, along with my grandsons. Jack, Sam, and Cole.

To my sister, Kathleen Naughton Connolly, her late husband Michael Connolly, and my nieces Joanne O'Connor, and Kathleen Carnelli, and my nephews Michael and Sean Connolly, and their children.

And finally to all my East Hartford friends and classmates, many of whom are mentioned in this book.

May God bless all!

Preface

To my readers:

This book along with my others, *Jump In and Start Swimming, Relationships Open Doors, Whatever Happened to the Pecords?* and *Heaven Sent,* plus the newspaper article of my trip to Woodstock 1969, complete my "How To Live Forever Series" in that they preserve parts of my life and careers in my own words for future generations to read. They will also serve as examples for my Baby Boomer-era readers to consider when writing down their own as well.

Of course, my books are designed to also entertain, so I provide real-life experiences for this purpose. It's also my intention to remind younger readers that even though you may be in a difficult situation (as you will read, I had many), you can become successful.

The stories of my humble beginnings, growing up poor in a project, having a difficult time in school, plus poor SAT scores that would block most from attending college are some bits of evidence that I share of how it went for me--and where it all amazingly ended up.

Note: If you're OK with just publishing your story as an electronic book (E-Book), Amazon Kindle (KDP) will allow you to publish your story for FREE! And it can be done in 25 minutes. You could also possibly make a few extra dollars in retirement if your story is interesting to the public, Note: It's a suggestion, not a requirement that you get copyright from the government. You don't need one.

That's right, my descendants and yours, a hundred years from now will be able to read about us and our family's life, not from a stranger's perspective, but our writing, in our own words, and will cost you zero, nothing, nada. It's the telling of your or your family's life story or a particular personal experience in your own words and publishing it that allows you to "live on forever." If you're a king or queen or president of a country it will be done for you. The rest of us need to do it ourselves!

I know what you're thinking. "This is going to be complicated." It's not. Each of us will have unique stories about ourselves or a family member, we might want to preserve. I have several stories (books), with two more in the works. My most recent, "Heaven Sent" is only about twenty-five pages. Yours can be as brief as three or four pages.

Note, I am not suggesting you write anywhere near as much as myself. This is my hobby. You just need to write down a few pages of your story similar to my friend's story below and then have one of your grandkids help you put up on Amazon as an e-book for FREE.

Maybe your father was in World War II or owned his own business or your mother has a story you would like to preserve. Just write it down the same as if you were telling it to a friend or relative. It's that simple.

For example, my childhood friend was born in England. I knew this growing up. I just didn't know the rest of the story until we were both much older.

Briefly, my friend's father was a 19-year-old paratrooper with the 509 Infantry Airborne Regiment during World War II. He saw a lot of action in Anzio and other major battles. (My friend might or might not want to elaborate on the action his father saw when he wrote this story down.) He was flown to England south of London which was being heavily bombed by the Germans at the time. The US had a hospital based near Portsmouth and while his dad was recuperating, he met a volunteer English nurse who took care of him. A romance blossomed and my friend was conceived.

His dad realized that the bombing was now spreading down the coast toward Portsmouth as he was getting ready to reunite with the 509, so he decided to move his bride and newborn son via a returning troopship to relatives in the US. Not easy, as the German U Boats were lurking nearby. There's more, but you get the drift. This is a story that should be preserved FOREVER.

If you have questions feel free to email me at info@keypublishing.com. My book website is KeyPublishingCompany.com. You can read a description of each story there or at Amazon.com

All of my books in addition to offering business and career advice, or providing entertainment, tell a story of my or my family's life that will surely live FOREVER. My newest story "Heaven Sent" has been released. "The Greatest," late this summer, hopefully.

I am available for speaking engagements Colleges, High Schools, Clubs, Senior Centers, Retirement Conventions, and anyone who wants to LIVE FOREVER!

Again, these are also life stories that will LIVE FOREVER! You can do the same with your own personal or family story. Don't worry about the length. If it turns into a novel, great if it's three, four, or five pages, so be it!

Just write it as if you were telling it to me over a cup of coffee and read my introductions on my book website, *www.KeyPublishingCompany.com.*

Jim / James P. Naughton at Key Publishing Company: I will speak to anyone who wants to LIVE FOREVER!

Contact email: *info@keypublishing.com*

Contents

Witness Protection Program

INTRODUCTION

My friends would often say, "Naughton, you always have a story about something." It is true; I always seem to, and "THEY DO TOO," although not everyone thinks to write them down. After all, we grew up during the '50s, an era of no television, well at least at the beginning of the decade., and no iPhones; this bestowed great imaginations on many of us. The radio also forced us to imagine. I have been telling stories since first grade, but just never had the time to write them down until I retired. My first book *Jump In and Start Swimming* was written for students at URI during the 2009 Economic downturn and subsequent job market collapse. In addition to stories, I have written a college job guide and articles for my hometown newspaper, The Gazette. For the 40th anniversary of Woodstock, I wrote about what I refer to as my "Forrest Gump" trip to a dairy farm in Bethel, New York, August '69.

This book in addition to being a part of my "How To Live Forever Series" is also a second sequel to *Jump In and Start Swimming*, in that it fills in the time after high school '62 and describes the period between college graduation '70 and landing my first career job at the Travelers

Insurance Company. Once again I "just did it"; I left for the Cape without any guarantee of job prospects. Yep, I "Jumped In," somehow knowing things would turn out positive and they did!

Like my others, it invites readers into another era and a chance to learn from my experiences as well as being entertained.

I was going to title it "The Adventures of a Baby Boomer." Because as I thought about it, every day seemed to be an adventure during the '50s and '60s. You may also note, especially when reading my *Whatever Happened to the Pecords?* I loved that era, especially the music, In the Still of the Night— Sho doe and Shubi do, Sho doe and Shubi do in the still of the night!!" I know it's crazy but I still get a charge and the urge to get up and dance whenever I hear these oldies.

All my stories are designed to entertain and also to motivate a younger audience that may have doubts about their prospects for a better life. I have learned so much from reading about others both from their mistakes and their accomplishments, maybe there is something you can learn from mine.

You will also discover that a lot of my memories are associated with the oldie songs of my era and I present them throughout the book. They help me to remember.

So... "Stay just a little bit longer, Please, please, please..." (Maurice Williams & The Zodiacs, "Stay," 1960).

As mentioned it's also an example of the "HOW TO LIVE FOREVER" campaign that I have started. Take an event or time in your or your family's life and write it down.

Could be long or short, and don't worry about character building or great adjectives describing a scene, as you are just telling a personal or family story from the heart and once you put it online at Amazon or Barnes Noble you will have enabled your great-great-grandchildren on and on, to learn about you and your family in your own words.

The beginning of this book contains a lot of what I refer to as "my life flashbacks," to periods from the early '60s through 1971. As stated earlier, "with my previous books I utilize these flashbacks to give you, my readers, a window to peer into and allow you to gain a better understanding of the era that my stories take place in."

Often the flashbacks are stories in themselves. Like in your lives, flashbacks do not always occur in a defined order, they just pop up! Often it's when "they" want to. Like this one!

1964 Corvette - $4037-sticker

It's about 4:30 pm, the sun is still high and hot this August afternoon, and once again I'm standing in front of O'Neill's Chevrolet on Rt. 44 in Avon, Ct. I just left HELCO's (Hartford Electric Light Company) nearby Hopmeadow Facility located at the bottom of Simsbury mountain and the famous Heublein Tower where I worked as an apprentice lineman.

I find myself here often after work, daydreaming about owning a 1964 Midnight Blue Corvette Convertible (Cost $4,037) prominently displayed in their showroom window. It would take me a hundred years to pay it off, I figured. One of our senior foremen, "Murph," owned one; why couldn't I? (I learned years later he was the uncle of my East Hartford High school '60s era star football player, Clayton Murphy.) I was also coming off serious illness and was considering the possibility of going to college full time. I naively thought "If I go back to school it will be years before I could own a car like this." I was also dating a nurse from the hospital, and where was all that going? All these decisions and conflicts are easy to comprehend and figure out now. Not back then! Not at 21!

A HELCO roving foreman pulled up in his truck and parked alongside a line crew working out in the country, giving them the go-ahead signal to head back early for the end of the day, while simultaneously bending down to pull up the metal ground pole attached to the wire spool.

"Jeez," "What caused the flash of light?" Crash!! Oh no!! Screams!

My God! A strong wind gust struck a quarter mile down the road—a fluke—knocking the recently hung loose replacement wire into an existing wire containing 13,000 volts!

The foreman was killed instantly. He was just being a decent boss, He didn't have to leave his truck to pull up that ground pole.

I said goodbye to my Corvette dream and enrolled in college, full time!

Chapter I

*Five years later, June 1970: College graduation,
driving to the "Cape" for R&R and a Summer job;
reminiscing, and flashbacks of my young life begin*

It was late June in 1970. I just finished college
and looked forward to some R&R on Cape Cod.
Staying in school through June became a necessity
because I needed a few more credits to get a
diploma which wasn't actually awarded till 1971.
I am already in my car heading to the Cape. If you
read my book *Jump In and Start Swimming*, you
would know that's what I do.

My life has a history of spontaneity, as you
will read in the following story. In no way am I
suggesting that my young readers emulate any
of my adventures, but rather I hope you garnish
a few positive ideas for your future use while
enjoying my book.

Before I get into the stories, I would like
to provide some background information. I
graduated from high school in 1962 in the blue-
collar town of East Hartford, Connecticut. Its
major employer, Pratt & Whitney, employed
36,000 spread over three shifts.

Across the street was the Aircraft Federal

Credit Union where I worked after school since turning sixteen at the beginning of my sophomore year.

Previously, at age 15, I made the best coleslaw at the Lobster Trap on Main Street, and before that, I was a paperboy for the Hartford Times, as described in my book *Whatever Happened to the Pecords?*

I can't recall a time when I wasn't working. My friends and I were collecting bottles as early as 2nd grade. It was what it was! I did what I had to do!

The Credit Union was conveniently located at the beginning of my street, Colt Street. Working there was like working for a family business. Their employees had watched me grow up, as my family moved there to our first house in 1956, directly across from its parking lot.

Yours truly, standing out in front of the Aircraft Credit Union 1963.

I wasn't sure what I wanted to do in life. I just knew I didn't want to be in school. I almost left my junior year to join the Marines with other neighborhood guys-Jimmy Johnston, Doug Sweet, and more, who had already quit. My blue-collar neighborhood was located across the street from the famous aircraft engine manufacturer Pratt & Whitney. There was very little talk of college in my area as it was taken for granted that my friends and I would eventually be employed by P&W.

I had flunked Geometry twice and naively believed I would not be accepted into college. Fortunately, my English teacher Mr. Engel (now a Professor at Quinnipiac University) caught wind of my plans. He was the only one I thought showed any interest in my future.

He called me into his office and read me the riot act about my thoughts of quitting. I studied him, tall, skinny with a trace of an accent, thinking, "why does he care about me?" I listened to him and stayed in school. Mr. Engel and I exchanged books at Quinnipiac University in 2014. What are the odds? I mentioned his impact on my young life in my book *Whatever Happened to the Pecords?* Upon reading it, a classmate located him at Quinnipiac and helped facilitate a reunion for us on Campus, February 2014.

My "book signing" sponsored by Goodwin College is discussed at the end of this book.

Reunion with Professor of English, Leonard Engel.
Formerly East Hartford High School Teacher. February
2014, Quinnipiac University

Chapter ll

*After high school, hanging out in the blue-collar factory
town, East Hartford, Connecticut, early '60s,
then Boot Camp "Parris Island," February, 1964.*

*"I'm now motoring toward Rt 195 and Providence
continuing to the Cape."*

In thinking back to September 1963. I was
considering joining the Marines with a local tough
guy from Glastonbury, Ernie Verdone. Ernie ended
up getting called out of line and was given some
type of medical waiver. I never knew why. The
funny thing was, that later he ended up being
drafted by the Army and spent two years stationed
in Newfoundland. In any event, I "tongue in cheek"
considered Ernie as my bodyguard; now what was
I supposed to do?

After high school, from the summer of '62
through 1963, I continued to work at the Aircraft
Credit Union.

Many of my friends, including Billy White,
Jimmy Maloney, John Choquette, and Gerry
Ceniglio and others, had signed up for the Navy
Reserves for two years active duty and were either
in Boot Camp or sailing overseas.

As I mentioned I graduated in May 1962, it was such an awesome feeling, especially for a kid like me that hated school. I still remember the best party that evening; I was driving in my 1952 Dodge Ram 4-door sedan, 3570 lbs, and no power steering; can you imagine? Plus it was a fluid drive, meaning you sometimes had a choice to shift or not; it was manufactured between the clutch and the development of a fully automatic transmission, complicated. Jimmy Maloney was sitting shotgun with the address for the party, but no details. We had a few to choose from.

My 1952 Dodge Ram Coronet White Top and Silver Blue Exterior cost $150 in my senior year, 1962. I hit 2 cars simultaneously at Martin Park when I took one hand off the steering wheel attempting to return the wave to Al Ambrose, one of a bunch of guys who had paused playing basketball, as I was pulling into the park. The car was like riding on a bucking bronco!

Suddenly we were in a crowd of cars and kids

in the middle of a large cul de sac. It seemed that half the class was there; out onto a porch at the house in front of us came this gorgeous girl with dark hair. She seemed to be waving at everyone, like "this is it, the party is here, come on in!" I mean that's what we thought. I asked Jimmy, "Who is that, a movie star?" We were still a distance away, but he was pretty sure it was Tony Mudano. Suddenly it seemed that a policeman who was just off to the middle of the cul de sac was waving me over while I was asking Jimmy, "Who was she dating?"

Oh oh, a police officer in the center seemed to be waving me over. I got a little shook and in following his command, I ran over his foot with my no-power-steering Sherman tank of a car. Oooh! Ouch! Jeez! "I'm dead," I thought. Maloney had turned snow-white. I knew I was going to lose my license. The officer just peered at me for what seemed like an eternity in disbelief and finally said, "Keep moving." Whew! He must have had a steel-toed boot.

Little Eva and "The Loco-Motion" was blaring from Tony's hi-fi: "Everybodys doin a brand-new dance, now! Come on baby, do the Loco-Motion!"

And we thought we heard her say, "Hey the two Jimmys are here, let the party begin!" We heard later it was, "Oh no, these wackos almost ran over a cop in my front yard!"

In any event, she was super friendly and invited us in. Her older brother Billy, another former high school star football player, wasn't around. Tony was also the star cheerleader. It was the best party ever. I never saw Tony again, but that's the way it was.

That's life! You're with these kids for four or maybe twelve years since kindergarten for nine months each year, and it was over. Nothing stays the same.

As a result, I have written a significant remembrance of my East Hartford classmates and friends towards the end of the book.

I wanted to not only preserve my stories "Forever," but I also felt it appropriate to do a little of the same for all those kids that touched my life. I placed them after the book's last chapter.

"No more books and studies, And I can stay out late with my buddies!" (Gary US Bonds, "School Is Out," 1961)

We left Tony Mudano's party and ended up at Pam Duell's house, where we were greeted by her friend Rosemarie Hopkins. Those two were not only good-looking, but also lots of fun. I couldn't believe it when years later I heard Pam was a nurse in Vietnam.

[Note for my East Hartford classmates and other Baby Boomer readers: If you want to be returned to this era quickly while reading, you might want to Google and listen to a song that the Fascinators wrote in '59 about Rose "Oh, Rosemarie"—"Don't pass me by..." A great oldie!]

It's difficult at a young age to imagine the future for friends. For many of the "kids," it's taken fifty-eight years to finally catch up through reunions and the internet with social media, and sadly many have left us. RIP, Pam Duell, also Claudette Tremblay who recently passed, I thought she looked like Elizabeth Taylor in high school. I think of her when I hear the Everly Brothers sing "CLAUDETTE," 1958, written by Roy Orbison. RIP, Claudette.

Advice for my younger readers.

As you read my story, keep in mind that I have written about the importance of Relationship Building and Networking in my book *Relationships Open Doors,* and I'll discuss and summarize it for you towards the end of this book. If you're a senior in high school or college or a new job seeker, you have a great pool of contacts already in your fellow classmates and their parents. I had over 450 in my high school class! You need to access them.

Networking and relationship building are NECESSARY and the MOST IMPORTANT skills a student needs to learn in order to get a career and also to advance in one's career. [*Relationships Open Doors*, James P. Naughton: www.KeyPublishingCompany.com www.Amazon.com/books]

Chapter III

*The stag party, the wedding
and beginning thoughts of the Marines.*

Marines, and more thoughts, as I continued driving to the Cape, The radio was fading just after playing "Hey, hey, Paula, I wanna marry you..." (Ray Hildebrand and Jill Jackson, 1963)

The song reminded me that a lot of my classmates were getting or considering marriage soon after high school. I had never even gone steady by that time and I felt I had a lot to accomplish before I could settle down if ever. We are the same, yet we're all different.

I first started to consider the Marines after a stag party that I attended with local friends, Jerry Ceniglio and Jim Maloney. Afterward, Jerry wisely suggested we spend the night at his sister Joan's apartment in an Italian neighborhood in Hartford, Connecticut, rather than drive home. Joan was a newlywed and a new mother.

She and her husband Paul Polo conveniently lived down the street from the hall on Franklin Avenue [Home of Giant Grinder, and the Rocking Horse Restaurant, and the famous Italian Restaurant, Carbones], Hartford, Connecticut.

Two things happened that night. One made
me famous or infamous in the Cenglio/Polo
households. I woke up thirsty and went to the
refrigerator looking for a cold drink. Later on, we
all awoke about five a.m. to Joan's screams in the
kitchen. Someone drank the baby's milk. Oh oh!
"But I couldn't find any cola." I have never lived
that one down.

*L to R: Yours truly fresh out of Parris Island, Jimmy
Jordan, The Groom-Jerry Ceniglio. Billy White and Best
man Jimmy Maloney*

I did end up in Jerry's wedding party, probably
the only non-Italian in the wedding hall except
for his best man Jimmy Maloney; so I wasn't

completely ostracized. Two Irish kids, unreal! It seemed like an honor at the time. The bridesmaids all looked like runway models and Gerry's bride, Annette Licitra, topped them all, looking so beautiful. Maloney and I were ready for a party. Before it started, a couple of other friends decided to crash the wedding. Yep! The original wedding crashers!! Billy White and Jimmy Jordan. (Actually, Jerry, unknown to us, had previously told them to stop by for a drink.)

Being the only two Irish guys at the wedding, Jimmy and I begged them to stay, just in case—and they did!!

The wedding was a blast. Of course, in those days when they threw the garter to the single guys, it was like a sandlot football game, except rougher; unlike football, we were all drinking, which allowed the traditional garter event to border on a brawl. You had to be there to understand. RIP, Annette.

The second thing that happened that morning was Joan's husband Paul Polo walking out of the bedroom with his Marine Corps uniform on, apparently heading for a weekend drill. That started a discussion between us regarding the Marine Reserves. I liked the uniform! Naive back then? Of course. Did anyone talk or even know about a place called Vietnam? Nobody I knew did.

My uncle who always believed I should attend college also suggested that I do the Marine Reserves which would include six months of active duty plus monthly meetings and summer camp. He rationalized "if you like it after training, you can always re-up (meaning volunteer to stay in for three years) and gain the ability to negotiate a school and duty station. Otherwise, you can attend college while serving in the Reserves. I wasn't sure.

The day after President Kennedy was shot (November 22, 1963) by Lee Harvey Oswald, I along with the rest of the country was feeling a mix of sadness and patriotism, so I drove over to Hartford Reserve Center and joined the Marine Reserves.

Unbelievably, the next day November 24, Oswald was shot by Jack Ruby and it came out that Oswald was a former US Marine!! I was numb.

Chapter IV

Parris Island, "The Few and The Proud"
- Read before joining!

Thoughts keep coming and the traffic is
building as I make my way to the Cape.

January 14, 1964. I was on a plane by myself
heading for Parris Island, South Carolina. The first
stop was Charleston, South Carolina with a five-
hour layover before being bused to Beaufort, SC.
The Parris Island Transfer Station. My high school
friend Jerry Ceniglio was waiting for me with a
borrowed car. He was stationed on an aircraft
carrier in the Charleston Naval Yard. I remember
seeing my first palm tree and thinking how nice
the warm weather felt as we toured all over
Charleston and the surrounding area.

It was my first time away from East Hartford.
Later a shuttle arrived and transported me to the
Beaufort Depot. I dropped a coin in the jukebox
and the song "Oh How I Want To Go Home"(Detroit
City, by Bobby Bare), began playing. I didn't get
a chance to select it. Did the machine somehow
know what I was thinking? Someone else chose
"Memphis, Tennessee," by Johnny Rivers, a song
about a divorced dad trying to get through to his

six-year-old daughter Marie. By the end of that song, it seemed that many had watery eyes.

The DIs showed up with stern looks on their faces and took us by bus across a bridge over a foreboding swamp and onto Parris Island, the only way in or out!

It was late, and we all just flopped in our bunks at the receiving station. The following morning was filled with a multitude of tasks, the first of which was a haircut, rather a completed shaving of our heads. Humbling! And meant to be so.

We then marched with all our newly acquired gear to our assigned barracks in 3rd Battalion, affectionately nicknamed Disneyland, because it consisted of new brick barracks, whereas the other two battalions were metal Quonset huts or wood structures that seemed ancient. I began to think "This isn't going to be that bad."

Yeah, right!

At 5:00 am, we were jolted from sleep by three screaming drill instructors as they hurled metal trash cans down the squad bay's cement floor banging off our metal bunks. *Get up! Get up! Get the F*#@%* up, you maggots!* they howled. I remember asking myself, "How could you ever have volunteered for this?" "Was I crazy?" I further asked myself—and it was only the second day of ninety.

Each platoon had three Drill Instructors. Ours consisted of senior DI Staff Sergeant Brown: tall, black, with a mustache; and our junior DI Corporal Odachowski from Brooklyn, NY. A third DI was on his way. We ran every morning at 5:15 am. Then we were marched to the mess hall for breakfast. To my amazement, the food was pretty decent.

Afterward, we went back to clean up our barracks and then out to the obstacle course for some serious PT. We did every exercise known to man and then some, climbed ropes, walls and walked on raised logs on the brutal obstacle course to improve our balance, then did pull-ups, and learned martial arts.

About two weeks into it, we were ordered to stand at attention behind our bunks to formally welcome a new Junior DI, Sgt Strickland, to our platoon. Strickland was short, muscular and slightly overweight with squinty eyes and two fingers missing from his left hand.

My bunkmate John Herlihy from Boston had recently graduated from law school and passed the Massachusetts Bar exam, whispered to me, asking what was going on plus a few more questions. I looked over and said "For Christ's sake, Herlihy! I'm barely out of high school and you just passed the bar. What do I know?"

Oops! Mistake! Strickland heard us. He does a U-turn and comes to our bunk and grabs my belt buckle and checks it out. Then he leans way back and scopes out the squad bay north to south, and simultaneously karate chops me in the solar plexus. Down to the floor I went.

After an introduction by Staff Sgt Brown, we were told to march into the head (bathroom). The line to the urinal was extra long, so I decided to brush my teeth.

I noticed glancing in the mirror, Sgt Strickland's face staring at my back. I must have looked at him like I had a razor to his throat, and he sensed it.

I watched his finger beckoning me in the mirror. "Oh, oh! Here it goes," I nervously thought as I walked over to him. My stomach instinctively began to tighten. "Naughton, you may think you're a tough guy, but I have got to tell you if you don't change your tune, I will make Parris Island hell for you."

Mustering up a fake half—maybe a quarter, or maybe an eighth—of a smile while trying to produce a non-confrontational look, I nervously said, "Yes sir." And I stayed away from him for the rest of my tour.

The rest of the day was filled with classroom training and things like hand-to-hand combat. Bayonet practice was followed by one on one matches using pugil sticks (a four-foot pole with a type of boxing glove at each end). You just prayed your opponent wasn't three times your size, which happened occasionally. Learning to fire your rifle on the rifle range was an important part of basic training. Damn it, I made a mistake during training at the .45 pistol range, when I nervously turned to the DI as he yelled in my ear. *Crap!* I had the .45 at "raised pistol" meaning it was at a 45° angle, so as I turned, guess where it was pointing?

Yep! He began screaming in a blood-curdling manner, "He tried to shoot me!! He tried to shoot his drill instructor!"

At least three other DIs from nearby platoons grabbed me as he kept screaming, "He tried to shoot his drill instructor! He tried..."

In seconds I was made to run around my platoon of ninety recruits, yelling "I'm a shit bird! I'm a shit bird!" for at least half an hour. Do you think it's funny? Now it is, but back then, I thought I was going to be court martialed when we got back to the barracks.

One night, I could hear yelling coming from the shower room. Oh, oh! Sampson and Toomey, reservists from Boston, who were assigned to a weight platoon, got caught with a bunch of donuts in their pockets that they swiped while on mess hall duty.

They were made to wear their rubber rain ponchos and do "side straddle hops" with hot water spraying from the shower heads making a steam bath effect. You had to feel sorry for them. They looked like death the next morning, but they survived and lost a few pounds. They graduated with us.

We would be given multiple-choice exams every so often. It was all memorization, which I excelled at. I always scored in the top three out ninety in the platoon. Eventually, I was called in front of Staff Sgt Brown, our senior Drill Instructor. "Naughton, are you a college kid?" he snarled. *No sir,* says I! "Don't lie to me Naughton, you're a college kid, you just scored a 98 on the test." *No sir!* It suddenly dawned on me he doesn't like college kids. "OK, go back to your bunk, and you better not be lying to me."

I made sure I got a few wrong answers on the next exam.

Swimming training was another part of it all. What a shocking experience, when we watched them push some recruits, non-swimmers, into the deep end of the pool. Mind you, these guys raised their hands when they were asked "Who can't swim?" They let them drown, or close to it.

Then they pulled them out with long poles that had a type of body hook at the end. Of course, the vision of watching the DIs sadistically screaming in their ears as they pulled them semi-conscious up to the surface was just crazy. *[Make sure you take swimming lessons BEFORE you report to PI.]*

Marching practice was a daily event. Our Platoon 309 won the "Boot" for the Battalion marching competition. We were the best marchers in the 3rd Battalion. It was the only time I can recall the DIs smiling.

It was, go, go, nonstop, all day, ending with another run around 4:00 pm. Woken at 5:00 am, lights out at 9:00 pm, Monday through Saturday.

On Sundays, we got an extra hour of sleep and attended church services. It was not, however, a day off. Just slightly easier. We played soccer and other physical games. Some guys passed out from exhaustion. Yep, even on Sundays. Except for some recruits from New York, most of us had not even seen a soccer ball, let alone played it, in that era.

In early February we were put on alert due to Fidel Castro's turning off the water supply to Guantanamo Bay! Nothing came of it, at least for us.

By the second month, training seemed to get easier as our bodies and minds began to acclimate to the rigorous schedule. I was able to send and receive a few letters from Hazel, a pretty girl from the north end of town that I was dating during the fall of '63. She was a super nice kid and her letters helped me to escape the tension of PI for a few minutes. It just wasn't meant to be.

We were given full physical exams by Navy doctors, then taken to a state-of-the-art dental facility staffed by some excellent Navy dentists. When you left PI you were in the best shape in all facets of your life. During the third month, we were marched out of the battalion grounds to a barbershop. We were allowed to have a little bob in front which was welcomed after being bald for two months. A sign that we were getting close to graduation day.

NOTE TO MY YOUNG READERS: If you decide to join the Marines, my suggestion is to spend at least two, possibly three months getting into shape before showing up on Parris Island. That's right, "Be in shape, to get in shape." Run for 2 to 3 miles, do pull-ups, practice climbing ropes if possible. You will thank me!

Another sign!

Marching out past 3rd Battalion and down the main road, as we passed a gas station, Milstead, a kid from Alabama, kicked me in the butt and whispered, "Naughton, what is that?" Of course, if a DI ever caught you talking, it would be Lights Out.

Then I heard it. A song from a radio blaring from the gas station on our left. "I wanna hold your hand," with a British accent. "How would I know?" says I, from the corner of my mouth. Milstead went back to quietly singing "Soldier Boy"!

Thinking back, the music and everything else was changing. "Happy Days" was quickly coming to an end. I didn't know it then. But I had heard the Beatles for the first time!

"So Bye, Bye Miss American Pie, Drove my Chevy to the levy, but the levy was dry..." Don McLean's song about the end of our Baby Boomer music due to the deaths of Buddy Holly, Ritchie Valens, and the Big Bopper in a plane crash into a Minnesota cornfield. The "whiskey and rye" line is a reminder that too much of it was consumed back then. I'm not going there with this book. Just wanted to acknowledge it was a problem for many.

Some escaped, some didn't!

My mother drove to Parris Island with my sister Kathleen to attend my graduation, April 1964.

A few nights before graduation I was given a two-hour fire watch from 12:00 am to 2:00 am for the barracks next door. The smell was almost unbearable. I didn't know where it was coming from.

I found out a couple of weeks later when we got to Camp Geiger for Infantry training. A

Corporal said "You smelled fear." He continued that it would have been the same smell I would have smelled if I had just walked into our barracks the first couple nights at PI. I never forgot it!

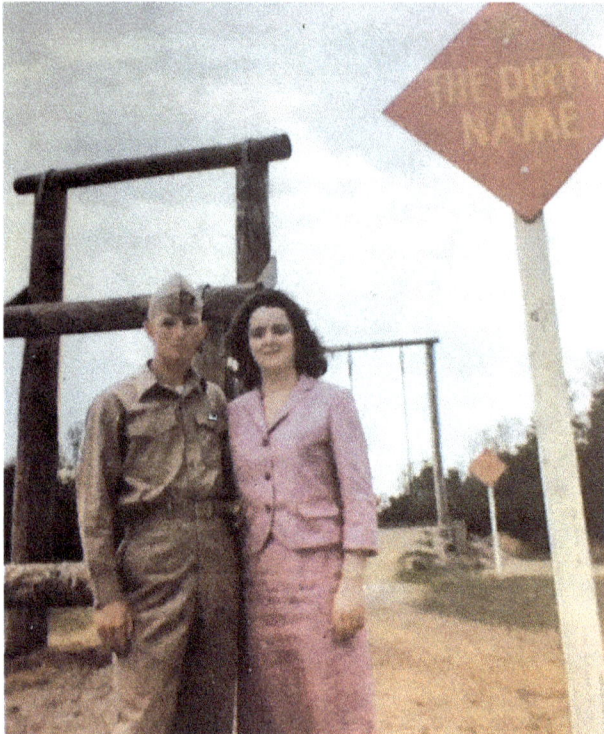

My sister Kathleen with me at the Obstacle Course, PI Graduation- April 1964. When he was making house calls Dr. Murphy, who just about everyone at St Mary's had as their family physician would enter our home singing "I'll Take You Home Again Kathleen" by Bing Crosby. He would sing the whole song if my sister was there!

We graduated on April 16, and I had never felt in better shape in my young life. I believed I could do anything. To my pleasant surprise, my mother and sister Kathleen showed up for our graduation ceremony. They had driven down from Connecticut. This was a big undertaking back in the day, but I was so glad to see them.

Yours Truly, directly behind SSgt WAL Brown

Our 2nd DI, Sgt Strickland, who had karate chopped me in the stomach early on, was suddenly treating me as his best friend. Turned out he wanted me to introduce him to my sister Kathleen. *Sure,* says I. *Not in a million years,* I silently thought—but I still had a couple of days and had to play the role.

He never mentioned it again, nor did I. The next day we were on buses heading to six weeks of infantry training at Camp Geiger, near Camp Lejeune, North Carolina

Here we are again—the rest of the photo.

After Camp Geiger, we went home for a two-week leave. Upon return, rumors were flying around about a country called Vietnam. I admit I wasn't that well-read, so I had never heard of it. My guess is that neither did the rest of the platoon. The rumors suggested that it was a dangerous place. They marched us out to a forest on what felt like the most humid day of my life. "Bam!" "Bam!" Suddenly, everything started exploding around us.

When it was over, we listened to a Sergeant over a loudspeaker shout, "Welcome, Marines, to Vietnam!" (I will never, ever forget hearing those words.) Then on cue from the top of a nearby tree, a vicious looking ball of pointed sticks wrapped with vines came crashing down swinging on a rope, narrowly and intentionally missing our platoon.

We soon learned that it, along with what were referred to as punji sticks, were part of the Viet Cong's crude homemade weapon arsenal.

The sergeant who appeared out of a crudely constructed Viet Cong village explained how they would create a booby trap by digging a hole about a foot deep and place these pointed "punji sticks' soaked with human pee and excrement. They could pierce our boots and cause a life-threatening infection. This was a real wake-up call!

My plans to "re-up" (to stay in), with a guaranteed duty station, school, etc., started to look probable as news that North Vietnam had begun helping the Viet Cong in late May was reported. Then came the Gulf of Tonkin incident in August '64. It involved one real and one falsely claimed confrontation between ships of North Vietnam and the United States in the waters of the Gulf of Tonkin. Originally the American report blamed North Vietnam for both incidents, but years later, the memoirs of Robert McNamara's publications from 2005 proved material misrepresentation by the US government to justify a war against Vietnam. It appears we were going to get activated anyhow. No one cared. We were young, we grew up with GI Joe, played Army as kids and no one ever really died.

We began to notice that at each monthly weekend drill meeting, gray-haired men and women were showing up and Taps was played at the beginning of each Reserve meeting.

It didn't take long to realize that these were parents and their kids were getting killed. A bunch of us naively signed a letter volunteering to go over, if we could remain as a platoon.

Soon after the Gulf of Tonkin incident, we had to fill out all kinds of paperwork that seemed to indicate that we would be activated, however, Congress suddenly passed a resolution stating that you could not activate the reserves during an undeclared war (It was called a Conflict). Looking back, with a 3.5 Rocket launcher MO, I'm told that my life expectancy was about 45 days. It wasn't meant to be.

Bobby Beaman from Mayberry Village, East Hartford, missed a reserve meeting and was immediately drafted. He was soon killed during one of the only amphibious landings on a Vietnam Beach—Horrible!

It was rumored that the Captain who drafted him, an executive at the Travelers, went into a deep depression and ultimately resigned. Every so often I wonder about Milstead, another bunkmate, Williams from West Virginia, and the others who made up the regular portion of our platoon. There were approximately 45 regulars and 45 reservists. What happened to them?

I guess that 90% of them were sent to Vietnam. There isn't a website that I can find for Platoon 309 and it seemed morbid to look up names when visiting the Wall. Like me, they had no idea what they were about to head into. I always offer a silent prayer for them. Sometimes I feel like those people who survived an airplane crash, confused, even guilty to a degree!

Chapter V

Home from boot camp, hanging out with the boys.

"Lots of traffic heading to the Cape. It's gonna take me a while."

Ernie died young. in his early thirties, of a brain tumor, while I was living out of state. I remember thinking "How young!" and becoming very emotional. The Marine medical examiners must have noticed something.

I always thought Ernie saved my life one Friday night as we, Jimmy Maloney, Billy Carbone, Bobby Menger, Jimmy Jordan and some guys from The Willow Inn (I discuss the Willow Inn later and how the Willow became my college campus) went to DeLisa's on Wethersfield Avenue in Hartford.

DeLisa's was a little more upscale, with a piano bar, than our regular haunts. It was considered the premier nightclub of its day in the greater Hartford area.

Billy Carbone started chatting with a pretty blonde when suddenly her boyfriend, a Hartford tough guy, came in. He charged down the four steps and immediately slapped Billy across the face and proceeded to go around our circle slapping everyone.

I was last in the line so I knew what was going to happen, and no way I was going to get slapped! I clenched my fist and sucker-punched the jerk before he could raise his hand, which allowed all of us to jump on top of him. We didn't see his bodyguard, a giant of a guy, coming in.

The guy wanted to kill me, but Ernie, who was just walking in, would not have it. His father, a union man, was well connected and was able to prevent me from being destroyed just before the cops showed up.

These stories and the following are not an attempt to brag or glorify anything, but just to paint a picture of what it was like for a blue-collar kid attempting to get into and graduate from college while living off-campus in a blue-collar town during the '60s. As you read on, you can tell it wasn't a normal college experience for some of us. RIP Ernie!

"I cried a tear, Because of you..." (LaVern Baker, 1958). "It seems like everyone is on vacation and heading to Cape Cod, so I keep on reminiscing." and listening to "Party Doll," Buddy Knox, 1957: "... To be everlovin' true and fair, To run her fingers through my hair."

Upon returning home from Camp Lejeune, I resumed working for the Credit Union. After a few weeks, I requested a meeting with Mr. Olsen, who was president of the Aircraft Federal Credit Union, to see what my banking career opportunities might be. He was approachable and understanding, but the bottom line was that I would need a college education to advance.

No way was I going back to school! I bided my time.

Chapter VI

Thinking back on our trip to the World's Fair,
Summer, 1964

Midsummer '64, I was still recuperating from
boot camp and I went with my childhood friend
and St Mary's alumni Jimmy Maloney and Billy
Carbone to the World's Fair in New York. Billy, a
good-looking Italian kid from East Hartford, had a
bit of droop in his left eye which made him look a
bit intimidating. No one gave us any sh*t.

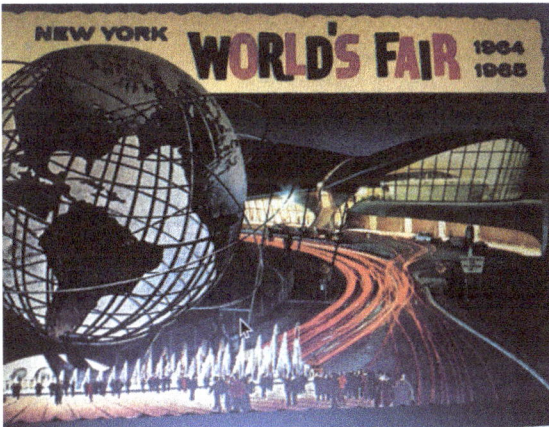

We had a blast! We met model and movie
actress Halle Saunders and her friends at one of
the many nightclubs and she taught us how to

do the "Monkey" on stage as the band played "He was spreading a new dance all around—Doin' the Monkey, yeah!" ("Mickey's Monkey," Smokey Robinson and The Miracles, 1963).

Suddenly her gown malfunctioned and fell to her waist! I remember the bass player patting his forehead with his handkerchief. The saxophonist dropped his instrument. Billy said to keep on dancing, so we did.

In case you didn't grow up in the era, when doing the Monkey you swung your arms one after the other up above your head and down toward your knees. That was it; that was the Monkey, simple and everyone was doing it. Jimmy saw a backup table cloth hanging near the stage, grabbed it, and threw it over Halle's chest.

The small audience thought it was part of the act and began clapping, hooting, and howling.

The World's Fair was never the same after our visit. We weren't 21, but it was no big deal, as the legal age in New York was 18. The next night we were at a nightclub called the Peppermint Lounge, we watched Joey Dee and the Starlighters sing, "The Peppermint Twist."

Outside the club, talent scouts noticed a couple of local city girls from Washington Heights singing while waiting in the long line in front of the club. They were soon given a contract. Ronnie and the Ronettes, "Be My Baby." Unreal! We were there. Lots of fun. We laughed all the way home.

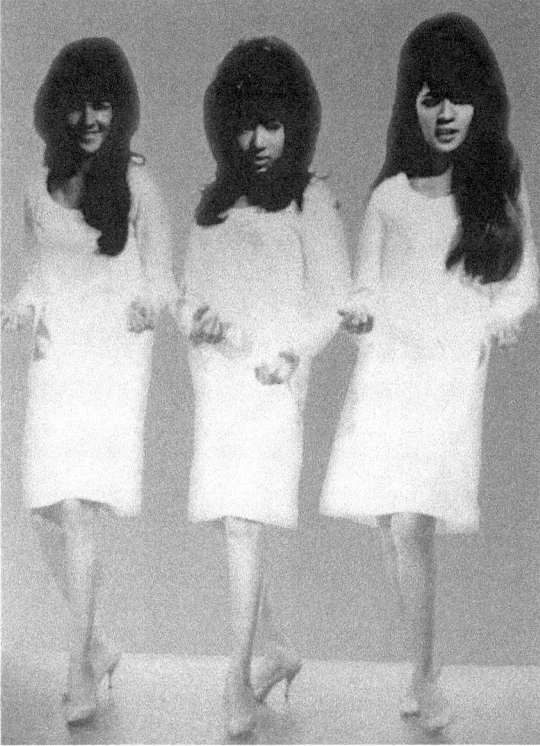

The Ronettes "Be My Baby" First heard at the Peppermint Lounge with the band Joey D and The Starlighters ("The Peppermint Twist"). New York Radio DJ "Murray the K and the Swinging Soirée," a "Blast from the Past," called them the "Be My Baby Girls"! You got to love their hair-dos. "The night we met I knew I needed you so, And if I had the chance I'd never let you go... " ("Be My Baby").

Chapter VII

*My first full-time job after high school,
first as a meter reader and then an apprentice lineman.*

*The traffic heading toward the Cape was now
bumper to bumper. The thoughts of the past keep
coming, along with the oldies: "Oh, oh, what a night;
It was, it was such a night..." (Elvis).*

Someone told me about the great income that
an electric power lineman could earn. I wasn't
afraid of heights, but to get hired, one had to
first become a meter reader. The meter reading
department was a type of pool from which you
could watch for various job openings. So that's
what I did.

I applied to Hartford Electric Light Company
toward the end of the Summer of 1964 for a
position as a meter reader and got the job. You
were given a different route each day, along with
a company car, and off you went. Returning each
afternoon with all the customers' meter cards
filled out which would determine a customer's
monthly bill.

They gave us uniforms with a long heavy
flashlight and mace. Everything went smoothly
most of the time, then one afternoon working a

route in Manchester, Connecticut, I had to read a meter which was in the kitchen.

The owner let me in and I noticed a small dog barking in an iron cage. Yikes! He broke out, jumped in the air, and grabbed the sleeve of my company jacket, which thankfully seemed to be made out of steel fibers. I could not get it to let go. There I was, walking around the kitchen trying to shake the growling dog off my arm. The woman was yelling, "Don't hurt Fi, Fi! Please don't hurt Fi, Fi!" while I'm thinking, "It's going to break through my tough jacket and rip my arm." I finally slammed it against the wall, hard. It slid down motionless and I quickly exited the home, expecting to be called into the boss's office when I arrived back to headquarters in Wethersfield. Never heard a thing.

A couple of weeks later, again in Manchester, I was moving quickly, jumping over hedges (When you finished your route you were done for the day, so you tried to move fast.). This one hedge was tall, but I cleared it. I was still in great shape coming out of PI. *Bang!* Right in front of me was what looked like a cross between a Great Dane and Rottweiler with a huge chain attached to a metal pole. I startled it and it jumped toward me breaking the chain. *Oh oh!* I noticed that it was a heavy-duty chain that you could pull a truck with.

Quick to the draw, I was instantly able to maneuver the extra-long flashlight into the beast's open jaws. I quickly pulled it out and nailed him across the snout. It gave me barely enough time to scramble over a fence on the far side of the yard.

Everyone at work wanted to see the teeth marks on the flashlight. I did get called on the carpet for that incident, but it was quickly resolved.

A little over a year before, another meter reader had ended up with twenty stitches from that monster. Afterward, I became a bit of a hero for my quick action.

In another incident, I was in the basement of an older home in South Windsor, Connecticut. I notice some skeletons of large rats near the wall. I kicked instinctively when my flashlight lit up a good size rat sitting on my boot staring up at me. Unbelievable!

Finally, on one hot summer day, while working in the north end of Hartford, I was walking down a basement corridor of a large apartment building in a tough area of the city. Each apartment had a storage area constructed of ship-lock boards with three-inch spacing, so you could see through almost to the back of the basement. I could see the rows of meters in the distance; then I heard a commotion. Flashing my light toward the left far end, I could see what looked like a mattress, a girl holding a dress, and some guys. I pretended not to notice and began reading the meters.

All of a sudden I hear a female voice, "Hey, boy, come on over!" My light caught a glimpse of a guy, his back pressing up on the slats, easing my way, along the wall toward where I was standing. At the same moment, the girl's voice again said, "Come on boy, no one is going to hurt you." *Oh yeah?,* I thought. I immediately put my head in a boxing stance; with my flashlight in one hand, the mace in the other, and I yelled "Damned straight, no one is going to hurt me!" while running like the dickens out of the place.

My boss didn't like it when I called and refused to continue working in that neighborhood. Fortunately, a position for Lineman Apprentice came open and I applied. I couldn't wait to leave the meter reading.

At 5'7", I was a little short, but they overlooked it. I think it was because I did so well in the mechanical aptitude test. Height was significant because you often had to lean back once at the top, to make connections. If you were short, you would have to climb higher, and bucket trucks were still a novelty. Thus, I began my new career.

At first, I was driving a large line truck, room for two in the front, and three to four in the back cab with a counter opened to us in front. It allowed for some serious card games during lunch. I had zero experience driving this huge truck and everything was on-the-job training. Still, driving down Simsbury Mountain in a 20-foot line truck, towing a forty-foot light pole in the back, and having to double-clutch the gears with a total of five or six of us inside was a little scary. The guys didn't seem to mind as I burnt out clutches and ruined gears in the beginning. They were concentrating on Gin Rummy. Luckily I knew how to drive a stick shift, but that was in cars.

Suddenly I heard a crash outside. Through the large side-view mirror, I could see a lunch box emptying out on the road. "What the heck, I thought?" My foreman, Roamy, said not to worry and explained that Joe, one of the lineman, was pissed because his wife only included one pack of cigarettes in his lunch box. She was supposed to include two.

No kidding? Joe had been stationed in Guadalcanal during World War II and married a native. *"I am a lineman for the county And I drive the main road…" (Glen Campbell, "Wichita Lineman")*

In addition to not having a fear of heights, one of the guys said you had to be a little crazy in this trade. Really? I found out later that Roamy, my foreman, was married to my high school friend Ray Ramsay's aunt. "What are the odds?"

After a week I mastered the truck and everybody seemed to like me and I was making good money. When the married guys passed on weekends for on-call duty, I volunteered. I took any time available. I soon graduated to a C Lineman where I could work on 120/220 volts. Everyone was supportive. Murph, a giant of a man, took me under his wing. I learned later he was my classmate Clayton Murphy's uncle!

A lineman from East Hartford introduced himself as Donnie Raymond and I quickly learned that he was an older brother of George and David Raymond who I had gone to St Mary's with. Once he found that out, we became good friends.

Great pay, great benefits. Can't have a fear of heights!

Soon after, Sonny Calabrese, a US Marine, also from East Hartford introduced himself and became a great mentor for me. I didn't know until this year that he was related by marriage to my King's Court friend Babe Pelletier Urso. It was probably one of the best blue-collar jobs of the era. (I realize I have written often stating that "I don't believe in coincidences, but I have had so many during my life that it's a quick way for me to acknowledge the unseen hand of God.)

After a while, I started getting a little too money-hungry, possibly due to growing up poor, and I took a part-time job at the supermarket that opened right where the United Homes used to be.

I can't recall the name, but it was like a Stop n' Shop located next to the Topps Discount store not far from the Coca Cola Company on Main Street.

Three nights a week and some Saturdays. A young 16-year-old Mexican kid from Hartford, Juan, would be sweeping the floors just before closing. One night just after nine I noticed him waiting for a bus up on Main Street. So I stopped and offered him a ride. He lived on Albany Avenue, Hartford, which was a pretty tough neighborhood in the era.

For some reason, I felt protective of him, possibly because we were both the first generation, so when he told me his family was on the third floor I figured I better walk him up. His mother was standing in the doorway holding rosary beads. His father was also there with his younger brother and sister. Yep, I took him home every night we worked together.

His mother didn't speak English, but she showed me her rosary and indicated she was saying it for me as well. I wondered whether sixteen-year-old Juan was their sole support. One night he begged me on behalf of his family to stay for dinner. His younger brother and sister brought me all their toys. They didn't have a lot. It was the first time I ever had Mexican food. Not bad! At

Christmas time I went and picked out a toy dump truck for his brother and a small doll for his sister. After a few months, I became ill and had to quit the store. I never saw Juan again. I have no idea as to where it came from, but from a young age, I cared about less fortunate people. Maybe 'cuz I was one of them.

I think I was born with empathy, like some are born with a gift to play an instrument or to grasp and understand higher math problems.

Feliz Navidad!

Chapter VIII

*Driving to "The Cape" for some R&R and a
Summer job while thinking of current news and
continuing to remember the past. United Homes
suddenly appears as a flashback.*

It's June 1970: I finished—graduated!! Now I
needed some fun. My dilemma was, I also needed
some income. I was in my mid-twenties and I just
couldn't afford to lie on the beach for a month.
Fortunately, I kept in touch with my lineman
buddies, Joe Pierce, and Kenny Rasmussen,
who upon learning of my dilemma, offered me
their rented summer cottage in Yarmouth on
the Cape. My next challenge was to find a job,
maybe bartending, for the rest of the summer
before embarking on some career about which, I
embarrassingly admit that I had no clue what to
do.

Originally I planned on being a high school teacher,
and I was even permitted to substitute teach on my
days off. Something changed in me while attending
college and I decided I wanted to look for a business
career. What? I wasn't sure. Besides, in case you
don't remember, the job opportunities were scarce
in the early '70s. It was not as bad as what we later
experienced in 2009, but it was very difficult. I

47

responded to my summer school Art professor when she inquired about what I planned to do. "That I just knew I was going to make a lot of money." She then asked, "How do you know?" I just shrugged my shoulders. "I just did," and **I really did!** Again if or when you read my first book *Jump In and Start Swimming*, you would understand that if you make the leap, Heaven will provide the net (It's called faith.). I'm not talking about jumping from one job to the next, but rather listening to one's intuition and making quick decisions.

Late June '70, I finished college and my last house painting job, collected five hundred bucks (not bad for the era), returned my rented forty-foot ladder, and headed to the Cape. I was always a worker bee. "Sweet Caroline," 1969, Neil Diamond, was playing on my car radio.

When I graduated in 1970, the average price of a house was $23,600 and the cost of a gallon of gas was thirty-six cents. Vietnam protests continued, as President Nixon allowed the war to spread, with US troops invading Cambodia.

A month earlier, four students were shot and killed while protesting the Vietnam War on the Kent State Campus by members of the Ohio National Guard. I couldn't believe it.

I mean... the year before I was still in the Marine Reserves! Could I have shot a college kid or any US citizen? No f'n way! Later, 100,000 protesters marched on DC. Imagine the students' parents. Imagine those young soldiers carrying that gruesome scene for the rest of their lives. I can't! I'm sorry, I just can't!

Then Paul McCartney announced that he was leaving the Beatles, making "Let it Be" their last album. It seemed longer at the time, but it was only six years since I first heard them singing "I Wanna Hold Your Hand" blaring out of that gas station on Parris Island. During that period I went through boot camp with the Marines, then began a career as an electric power lineman and just graduated from college. It's almost overwhelming to think about it.

(Please feel free to go to my book website *www.keypublishingcompany.com* and download a copy of my 1969 Woodstock article published in my hometown newspaper *The Gazette*. It will allow you a quick glimpse of the country through my eyes, as I personally witnessed events.)

From my perspective, it wasn't a great time in our country or in the world. Vietnam was a major reason: We ended up with 50,000 dead, and the average age was 19! Maybe that's why Simon and Garfunkel's song, "Bridge Over Troubled Water," led the charts.

I was very optimistic about my personal future even though the job market was sparse. I was done with school, finally. I was so excited I felt like I was going to explode. I knew everything was going to work out. It had to!

At the moment, I could not fully comprehend much of the news. I was just so elated to be done with school and finally at age 26 begin the next phase of my life. I knew I had to take a rest. I hadn't stopped once in years. While in college, I worked almost full time.

I arranged my classes often into the evening so that I could substitute teach (permissible in Connecticut during the '60s if one had a military ID, was 21, and attended an accredited college).

If I wasn't substituting, I was often an on-call beer delivery assistant for Budweiser. Evenings and weekends, I would often be working as a dispatcher for the Hartford Automobile Association: Triple-A. Just considering all the work I did while in college is exasperating!

Still, I was now in my mid 20s and needed money. So my "rest" would have to include a job, possibly as a bartender in Hyannis. It didn't yet dawn on me that possibly all the bartending jobs were already taken by the college kids who finished school in May. It was now mid-June. Back home my friend and fellow graduate John Choquette agreed to alert me to any job fairs that might appear in our local newspapers.

Continuing my drive to the Cape and more reminiscing. I know that these flashbacks are not in a particular order. That's just how flashbacks are!

The traffic was considerably heavy for a Monday evening in June and the radio reception was temporarily disabled, both of which caused me to reminisce. I was confident, but slightly nervous about the future. As I stated, the job market seemed to be in a stalemate, but I was single and rationalized that things would work out. I had always worked as far back as I can remember, beginning way back at age nine.

The fact that I was graduating with a class whose average age was 21 seemed like a positive. I thought "Maybe employers would consider me more worldly at 26?" I hoped the fact that I did not follow through with the teaching degree that I began studying for wouldn't be looked upon by potential employers as a negative. I also realized that I probably should have switched to a business curriculum, but I didn't want to spend even an extra day in school, so I continued with a major in English and minor in psychology.

As I motored toward the Bourne Bridge and Cape Cod my mind became flooded with more thoughts of the past and I remembered the United Homes Housing Project where I grew up until age twelve.

The dwellings were originally home for soldiers who during the war protected Pratt & Whitney Aircraft, the world's largest jet engine manufacturer just a few minutes south on Main Street. Thinking back, there wasn't a lot to them, small cabins with one or two bedrooms. They were made of plywood, no insulation thus it felt like you were in an oven during the summer.

In the winter we were kept reasonably warm with a kerosene stove set between the living room and small kitchen. Every family got a plot of land for a garden and were encouraged to grow potatoes and other vegetables.

As a kid, the best memories were of the many playmates we had. It was easy to gather five or ten kids in a matter of minutes for a game of baseball, hide and seek, etc. I still remember most of their names.

Yours truly in the United Home project.
It's in the book that I wrote for my motivational talk
"Jump In and Start Swimming" for URI. I also displayed
this picture to emphasize to seniors who were having a
hard time getting jobs due to the '08 economic crash
that ANYTHING is possible!!

Kids like Joey Peppin, who joined the Marines and served, and survived Vietnam; his brother Freddy, hit by a car crossing Main Street in second grade. He went on to become a star baseball player in town and eventually a celebrated Hartford policeman. You will note later on that they moved to King Court. Charlie Ekdahl and his sister Janet, Bobby Corriveau, Guy Christenson. Billy Griffin, and others lived in the project.

Many of my friend's families moved on to another famous project, Mayberry Village. We reunited in high school. Kids like my next-door neighbor, Christo Jamo.

Christo's parents had a homemade fire pit going most Friday evenings where we roasted hot dogs and marshmallows and listened to ghost stories. I loved it all. I could be living in a king's mansion and not have as much fun as I did in the United Homes. I have fond memories except for the oppressive heat in the summer and the thin walls of the homes that let much of it inside.

The traffic just got heavier, so I'd better keep my eyes on the road. I continued reminiscing.

By the time I was twelve, my parents had saved enough money to buy our first house for cash! Don't forget they landed at Ellis Island with only the clothes on their backs! So we moved to Colt Street across from the main entrance to Pratt & Whitney.

I immediately got my first real job, a Hartford Times paper route. I will let you read about my teenage life and adventures on Colt Street in my book *Whatever Happened to the Pecords?* (Amazon.com) Note: In my book *Jump In and Start Swimming*, in order to provide some inspiration to the URI students during the '09 economic collapse, I described how my parents survived and eventually thrived, considering that in the beginning, they had no savings! No Jobs! No Unemployment Insurance! No Social Security! No Nothing! And new to our country at the height of The Great Depression.

I use their experiences to show my audiences that in America anything and everything is truly possible.

Chapter IX

Matriculation - finally getting into college through the back door at age 22.

More reminiscing about my college experience as I continued driving toward the Mid Cape Highway.

I had helped John Choquette get a job at HELCO and we seemed to decide about the same time that we should try night school with the intention that if we did reasonably well, we would consider matriculating as full-time students. I had only recently learned that matriculation meant that we could get into college through the back door—meaning that if you took some courses and passed, you could then apply to attend college with a good chance of getting accepted regardless of your low SAT scores. A different way to get into college and a gift for John and me. Of course, HELCO paid for everything!

I smiled when I thought of our first evening class together, English 101, University of Hartford. The professor showed up to a packed class looking ornery like maybe he just had a fight with his wife.

He started piling book on top of book while

shouting out that these were books we needed to purchase and read for the semester, followed by the number of papers we had to write, etc. etc.

After twenty minutes he stopped and stared at us. Then he menacingly said, "I expect a lot of you will be lucky to get a C if you complete all this— and by the way, it's not too late to get a refund if you don't like what I just said."

I looked from the corner of my left eye at John and noticed the weird look on his face. I got up and quietly said "Let's go." It was like a scene you may have heard of with identical twins being able to read each other's minds. Without another word or discussion, we both walked up to the professor and asked for a refund. He seemed stunned that we so quickly took him up on his offer, but without hesitation, he filled out two slips. Probably figured "two less I will have to work with."

Nevertheless, I knew he was shocked at our abrupt acceptance of his offer, as was the rest of the class. *Hey!* We were from East Hartford and don't take any sh*t from anyone, including college professors! (That will soon change.)

On our way to locate the office, we bumped into a guy who was lost and looking for directions in the hallway. Turned out to be a new young professor of English, Peter Brazzow, from upstate New York. He said it was his first time teaching and he was hoping to have enough students sign up for his English 101 class. What were the odds? Yep, we did and each got a B, and I believe that was our 'entre' to matriculate as full-time students and change our lives. *"Coincidence?"*

Yes, our lives were about to do a three-sixty. In addition, a mutual childhood friend, Jim Maloney, just off active duty with the Navy, had already enrolled at the University of Hartford which gave us more courage to take the leap! I decided to enroll at Central Connecticut State College (now Central Connecticut University). John went to the University of Hartford, at least in the beginning.

"I am making good time and soon will be heading over the Bourne Bridge to the Mid-Cape highway which runs all the way to Provincetown."

"Big Boy Pete' was just finishing on the Cape oldie station, "The Joint was jumpin' on the corner (yeah-yeah), down on Honky Tonk Street (yeah-yeah), and out stepped a cat named Pete…" (The Olympics, 1960)

Another smile emerges across my face, thinking of me on the Central Connecticut Campus in New Britain, CT, alone for the first time. I walked into the Student Center, initially very self-conscious. I was rough around the edges and that was an understatement. At twenty-two! Many freshmen were seventeen. Five years now, at my age, means practically nothing: Five years in your early 20s is a big deal.

Two things caught my eye.

First, the pretty 8'x8' picture of the Homecoming Queen hanging from the ceiling, whom I met twenty-five years later, living ten minutes from our home in Rhode Island, Sue Stubitz.

(As you will note in all my writings, my life has been full of coincidences, I should mention again, that I really don't believe in coincidences; but using the word *coincidence* eliminates the need for a long explanation, and as I have said many times, I believe it's the unseen hand of God.)

The second thing I noticed as I proceeded down the aisle was a male student near the stage talking to a group of sorority sisters. He was wearing what I thought were strange slacks that flared out at the bottom like Navy deckhand trousers, only these were more classy, with stripes from the waist to the bottom. Also, his blonde hair was curling up about three quarters down his neck.

Hey, I was an ex-hard hat with a Marine Corps buzz cut straight out of "Happy Days"! By the way, within about three months, I was sporting bell-bottom trousers and much longer hair, and eventually a mustache.

As I continued driving, I thought, *"I watched times change right in front of me due to enrolling in college."* My buddy John, who was attending the University of Hartford, switched the next year when I told him I was only paying $95 a semester, plus books. No kidding!

There are lots of fun stories about our college experiences that I will expand on during my speaking engagements if asked, like how we got to the front of lines, got the best professors, survived, and graduated. Stories like our encounter with Dr. Denucci, a doctor who became a Biology professor, who said that he was probably going to end up flunking both me and John Choquette because of what he perceived as our know-it-all attitudes.

We ended up going for drinks and became best friends. He didn't give us the answers, but he helped two "older" guys get acclimated to college life and especially Biology, There are more. Just ask!

When I saw the dude with the weird-looking slacks and long hair, I did an about-face and left the Student Center, thinking that I might have made a mistake. Thoughts like, "maybe I was too old for this," began to creep into my mind, making me feel a little depressed. No sooner did I hit the street when I heard someone calling my name "Jimmy Naughton"!

The sun was setting in the west, and I was facing east. I could vaguely make out an individual walking toward me as the sun was glancing off him. I didn't know anyone at Central. It was primarily a teacher's college.

Suddenly, I heard, "Hey Jimmy, it's me, Tommy, Tommy Connolly." Tommy Connolly from East Hartford, my hometown? Tommy Connolly, who I went to St Mary's with since Kindergarten? It couldn't be! Sure enough, it was him. I couldn't believe it.

He proceeded to tell me that he, along with Ronnie Perham, who later started his own commercial cleaning company, Suburban Maintenance, was at the college along with Bruce Chamberlain, who I learned grew up at Pitkin Homes, a sister military project to my United Homes.

Next, I met Brian Hope, who later joined his older brother Brett's Construction Company. Eddie Satolino, a great East Hartford High varsity football player, joined, along with Eddie Arnold who went on to become a successful paper salesman. I had his sister as a high school teacher. Eddie's younger brother Jimmy Arnold passed away too young. I didn't know him well, but he was well liked by all. He was married to Carmella Distefano, a super nice girl. RIP, Jimmy.

Veterans Club, CCSU, 1968

Later on, John's younger brother Gregg, who was stationed in Germany with the US Army, returned home from active duty. Greg began attending CCSU on the GI bill as did most of the guys. He and his girlfriend would join us for lots of fun at the Veterans club dances. RIP Gregg.

As I was driving The song "Eddie, My Love" by The Chordettes just came on. "Please Eddie, don't make me wait too long. Please, Eddie..." What are the odds? I had haphazardly located an oldie station somewhere on the Cape!

As I got acclimated to Central and the Veterans Club, I met Denny Tillotson, another famous varsity athlete, for our East Hartford High School basketball team. I learned recently that Denny's best friend, Freddie Kurtz, graduated from Central. RIP, Freddie.

Everything was falling into place for my new college experience. My depression left, and I wasn't alone anymore. I couldn't believe the number of guys from my class at East Hartford High School who were at the college and returning veterans. Down deep, I knew everything was meant to be. I can't begin to explain how much Tommy Connolly and Ronnie Perham helped make my very difficult transition into Central Connecticut State University possible. I thank them, but it's not enough. I will probably end up writing another piece on attending Central Connecticut State College, now a University. For now, I will just say that it took me a couple of semesters to get acclimated to college.

I mentioned later that I lived at home and worked full time, so I did not have a typical college experience. The Veterans Club or Fraternity as I thought of it, kept me centered. Guys like Phil Mullen helped me with my English major, particularly with writing papers. Phil is now a Professor of English at a college in the Midwest. I have been trying to locate Phil for a while now.

I was also with many of those who had done a stint in Vietnam. I consider them all "stand-up" guys. Guys you could depend on, and I did. After class, we often met up at the Palmer House next door to the campus.

Again, we were older—definitely a different kind of college experience. One night I got into a tiff at the bar, with some local New Britain guys. It was broken up quickly by my Vet Club buddies just as the cops arrived. The guy and his friends were real wise asses, and the scene ended up with a lot of pushing and shoving. The ring leader threatened us and the police about calling his father or uncle who he said was the mayor of New Britain.

The punk's name was Paul Manafort. The same? I don't know. He seemed too young to be allowed in a bar that night.

On weekends, the Vets Club held some fun dances with some great local oldie bands. I even got to Daytona Beach for spring break; again, thanks to Ronnie Perham, Tommy Connolly, and Brian Hope. I'm not sure who was crazier, us, or the four years younger college kids. In my mind's eye, I can still see us pulling up in front of the Desert Isle Motor Inn after driving straight through for 25 hours. Our apartment was right on the beach. I mean you opened the door and stepped on the warm white sand while looking past the cars driving on the beach and watching bathing beauties jumping in the surf. That's right, cars could drive on the beach and cars could get dragged out to sea, and they did!

To the right of our beach door was a kidney-shaped pool surrounded by palm trees. I had never—other than Parris Island—been away from East Hartford. I thought I was in paradise and within minutes my mind was saying "Quit school, get a job and stay here forever." Not very mature thinking and of course that's what it was, a momentary fleeting thought. I later called home and my mother began telling me about the late spring blizzard that was hitting Connecticut. Brrrr! "I'm staying here!", I thought. This was Spring Break, 1968.

On the way home I told Ronnie that I had never seen the cherry blossoms in DC, so we pulled off the highway, and there in front of us, the city appeared to be on fire!

Coming towards us were several jeeps with tops down carrying Marines with crossed bayonets. *What the heck?* Tommy turned the radio to a news station that said "Martin Luther King has been assassinated." We almost landed in the middle of the riots before doing an immediate

U-turn.

We felt like idiots not being aware, but that's the way it was in 1968. If you get a copy of my Woodstock article on my book website *www. KeyPublishingCompany.com* or *www.Amazon.com*, you can also get an idea of what was taking place in the US and the world in 1969. I went all year round to college, which included taking summer courses, to be able to finish as soon as possible. Again I'm not suggesting anyone emulate any of this, "Just the facts, ma'am!" Just the facts!

Carol Ammon, who I didn't know, had graduated from Central with us in '70 and founded a pharmaceutical company. It was reported that she recently donated $8 million to Central. I heard that it is the largest donation in the college's history.

I did very well in my career. John Choquette

and my other friends did very well also. I mention this because if you're discussing college on a tight budget and tuition is a problem, remember that we paid $95 a semester.

I realize that was a long time ago, but there were schools, even then, charging in the thousands. Spending a ton of money, especially when you can't afford it, does not necessarily guarantee you going to own a pharmaceutical company. Do not overlook your state colleges and for some, spending two years at a community college might eliminate tuition concerns.

Here in Rhode Island, you can attend a CCRI for FREE for two years then transfer to the University of Rhode Island and some others. BTW, attending a trade school while in high school or afterward might be a better choice for some. Computer Technicians, Auto Mechanics, Electricians, Carpenters, Plumbers and Estheticians and more, are all in demand and can provide good incomes.

Speaking of success and choosing a college, I found out years later that a kid from town about four years younger—don't forget we were older when we started—was attending Central at the same time. He is now a famous member of the US Congress. Rep. John Larson.

My friend John Choquette got into local government and became Assistant Mayor in our hometown of East Hartford for many administrations and Mayors, one of which was

Tim Larson, whose older brother is John. John Choquette introduced me to Tim, and we quickly became friends. Tim is now a Connecticut State Senator, and in the process of being appointed as Commissioner of Higher Education. More so-called coincidences.

Chapter X

My unusual campus experience at the Willow Inn and Friday nights at the Kayrock.

My college experience was anything but traditional. I lived at home except for a couple of semesters when I had an apartment in New Britain, which meant that I was often found hanging out at the Willow Inn, around the corner from my house on Main Street.

The Willow Inn was owned by a former policeman, Frank Benettieri, who became famous when he survived a shootout while responding to a domestic violence incident in a South End housing project. He was perfect as a bar owner: great personality, huge guy, and an avid Red Sox fan. Frank was five or six years older than us.

The Willow Inn was a traditional men's bar. It was referred to as a factory bar because of its proximity to Pratt and Whitney Aircraft. Almost directly across the street from Willow Street which was the main entrance for the shop workers which included my father and also my mother and many of my friends' parents. In the fifties, it was called Russell's and I went there often with my father as a young kid. The United Homes where I first lived until 1956 was just a few blocks away. And it was common for kids to accompany their parents into bars in that era.

I loved watching the TV, as we didn't yet have one in our home, and I was mesmerized observing and listening to the many conversations.

The place made me feel like a big shot for some reason. Probably because I always walked out with money from the customers who I guess thought I was a nice kid. One of the barmaids back then, whose name I think was Ruthie, always gave me a dollar with a look of sadness in her eyes; apparently, I reminded her of her son around four years of age who was killed in the Hartford Circus Fire.

The Hartford Circus Fire occurred on July 6, 1944, in Hartford, Connecticut. It happened during a performance of the Ringling Bros and Barnum and Bailey Circus that was attended by 6,000+ people, with 700+ injuries, and 167 deaths. I was too young then to grasp the horror of it all. As I got older and learned more about it, I would get a sick feeling in my stomach thinking about her and her little boy. I still do. Of course, I never would have thought that in my twenties I would be using the bar, which was renamed The Willow Inn, as my college campus.

One of our friends, Ugo Benettieri, was Frank's younger brother and sometimes bartender. Ugo had volunteered for the Air Force and was selected for Air Traffic Controller School. He subsequently was sent to Vietnam. When he returned he became an Air Traffic Controller for Bradley International in Windsor Locks and worked part-time at The Willow. Many of the guys that I went to high school with also hung out there.

A career as an Air Traffic Contrller is one that some of my younger readers should consider. I emphasize it, because it's one that you might not be aware of. It pays well, and you seldom hear of layoffs.

As I said, it was primarily a men's bar. Saturdays, especially in the winter, saw many "Setback" games. I couldn't afford a dollar a point, but played anyhow, hoping I would win. I do recall betting $100 on the 1968 Dallas Cowboys/Green Bay Packers NFL Championship and losing due to the spread!

A hundred back then was probably close to a thousand today, and I was a poor college student. In my mind, I can vividly see some of our crew. Wayne Menard worked for the MDC. Carmine Salvatore worked for the famous Marco Polo Restaurant, where everyone congregated after our high school dances, now closed after sixty years, Bobby Blinn, major league baseball draftee from South Windsor, and Freddy Kurtz and his wild stories as a prison parole officer.

More on my college campus!

Dave Prince didn't play cards but was always in a pool game. He was a muscular kid (not due to weight lifting) and very tough. His naturally brown curly hair took a slight dip in the front, a carry-over from the '50s hairstyles. The Willow often got crazy. One night a strange looking guy came in looking for his girlfriend. He was carrying a rifle.

I was standing at the bar talking to Sheila, Frank's barmaid, when suddenly this guy pointed the gun at Prince.

Prince, who was genuinely fearless, dropped to his knees, ducking behind the pool table, and began winging billiard balls at the guys head. The police arrived and took the guy away with a large lump on his forehead.

Another guy fired a gun at Johnny Hollis who was stopped in traffic directly outside the Willow, striking his hand.

Sometimes In the early days, the Willow could be like a western saloon, with card games, fistfights, and occasional shootouts. RIP, Dave Prince. RIP, John Hollis. I know it might sound crazy, but I loved the action. Sometimes when you're in a situation, it could be months, maybe years when you can contemplate it. I mean life happens fast sometimes. Not me, not then, I knew I was in a fun crazy place, right then and there; I couldn't wait for the weekends, party time! Immature? Probably. Not everyone's cup of tea? I wouldn't trade the memories for anything. That being said, there is no question I wanted better for my kids. I think they got it!

Friday nights we would all head to the Kayrock Inn, Lake Pocotopaug in East Hampton, Ct.

Kayrock Inn, Lake Pocotopaug
(Looks quiet. Not in the early and mid-'60s!)

Those nights were jam-packed with 21-year-old guys and gals—or those with fake ids—looking to dance and meet someone.

One of the Kayrock Inn's great rock and roll bands in the era was from Bolton, Connecticut. Do you remember the Eldridge Trio? Yep, that was the band we all danced to every Friday night, often outside on the large balcony overlooking the lake, as they sang: "Money—That's what I want, give me money... (The Kingsmen).

It could be a crazy place. One Sunday afternoon, Bill Carbone, Jimmy Maloney, and I went there for an afternoon session. A tough guy from Manchester, Red O'Neil, who knew Billy, suggested as a friend that we get our asses out of there *ASAP*. Supposedly, one of the notorious Kayrock bouncers gave a rough time to one of

O'Neil's buddies, and he and a black guy named Jay Jay and some friends were planning to even the score.

We left and positioned our car across the street from the front door on Route 66, and watched in awe over guys being thrown or jumping through windows. Another Manchester guy waited to sucker punch anyone leaving the front door. There were quite a few.

Next thing, we saw the place surrounded by state police. We heard later that a few of the Manchester guys were recently paroled and were heading back to the slammer. Unbelievable! Billy's friendship most likely saved us some serious injuries.

Chapter XI

*More flashbacks for East Hartford stories
as I continue driving.*

In the early years, Billy Carbone would show up at Mickey's Drive-In with his signature white '56 Chevy, with a white convertible top. Everyone liked Billy—just one of those types of guys. He would often just disappear on us. When I asked him where he went, it was always to meet Patty McVeigh, a gorgeous girl from East Hartford who was a little younger than us. Patty had a cute sister, Kathy McVeigh, who attended the Newport Folk Festival in 1963 (might have been '64 or '65; Bob Dylan performed at all three). I was there with Billy White and some others. I'm just not sure which one!

Billy Carbone also hung around with Nick Serignesse, who ended up getting his law degree and setting up his practice in our town. Nicky, a few years back, began throwing East Hartford Fourth of July parties at his Alpaca ranch in historic Lebanon, Connecticut. The front of his house faced the town green, where we later watched an old-fashioned American fireworks display.

It was an opportunity to meet up with the old gang and relive "The Glory Days" like in Bruce Springsteen's song.

At one of these parties, a bunch of us were chatting about the early deaths of some high school classmates: Ritchie Rizzo, Rich Jepson, and Johnny (Harry) Overend. I'm talking about dying from drugs, soon after high school in 1962, when suddenly Al Ambrose strolled in with Johnny.

"Are you kidding me?" I yelled, and instantly we were all surrounding Johnny like he was an apparition. It was him, and he proceeded to tell us he was with Rizzo and Jepson when they passed, as we listened and stared with our mouths wide open. I hadn't even heard of marijuana back then.

Johnny survived a difficult time and went on to help other guys with their addictions. His first name is Harry. So why Johnny? No clue; it's usually a family thing. (Some of you might remember, in the early '70s, the comedian on the Ed Sullivan Show. Wearing a large black fedora and a huge cigar, his shtick was "just don't call me Johnson, youz can call me Ray, youz can call me Jay, youz can call me Ray Jay. Just don't call me Johnson!!" Raymond J. Johnson, Jr. (aka Bill Saluga).

Harry not only got treatment and was cured, but he also ended up running one of the best drug rehabilitation institutions in the US, Daytop of Connecticut, which evolved into the Daytop Program APT [Addiction, Prevention, and Treatment], Affiliates of Yale Psychiatric and

Addictions Division. Best that you order his book and life story *Blessed With Two Lives: A Story of Addiction and Recovery*, at *Amazon.com* and *Lulu. com*.

Jimmy Maloney and I were always hanging together, especially after graduation. We had gone to St. Mary's since Kindergarten. We were difficult to handle, according to some nuns (Not true, we were misunderstood!), and you can read all about ours and our buddy Frankie Grandi's antics in my book *Whatever Happened to the Pecords?* at *Amazon.com/books KeyPublishingCompany.com.*

Soon after high school and a stint in the Naval Reserves, Jimmy was dating a pretty blonde at the University of Hartford. That ended suddenly. Not skipping a beat, he shows up at another town pub, Foley's, with some cute girls he met at his new Pratt and Whitney job, Pat Nappi and Betty Parent, and some others, Betty was dating Brian Keenan, who Billy White became friends with at his Pratt and Whitney, mailroom job. The P&W mail room was run by Al Healy, who I met making deliveries on behalf of the Credit Union where I worked through high school.

The mail room also served as a spawning department, allowing its employees to watch for more permanent and better grade jobs in the main company. I introduced Bill White to Al and he was hired. Al met and married Jonilyn "Doll" O'Connor, a gorgeous girl who I first met at St Mary's. "Doll" was a year or two ahead of my class. Her nickname matched her pretty looks.

My Willow Inn friends and I would sometimes meet at Monti's across the street on Main and Willow Street, which was the entrance to Pratt and Whitney. It was owned by Frankie Grandi's parents. We then would all head down to the Blue Sands in Misquamicut. It was at Monti's where I can still imagine hearing Dave Melody singing, or rather attempting to sing, "Hooka Tooka," by Chubby Checker.

We were partying two or three nights a week, plus weekends. How did homework get done? I don't recall. Somehow it got done, mostly. Also, I worked close to full time during some semesters. *Don't do this!*

Again, I'm not recommending any of this to my young readers. Concerning grades, I did OK. I could have done much better. Upon reading this, it might surprise you that I graduated.

Denny Tillotson would be at the Willow Inn on Saturdays, available for a game of pool. I mentioned earlier that Denny was a star basketball player for East Hartford High and was also attending Central Connecticut State at that time.

Occasionally, Bernard Hopkins would pop in. I remember him from St. Mary's Kindergarten.

Like I have said many times, I might not remember what I did two months ago, but for whatever reason my memory going back fifty or sixty years is keen. Bernard and a kid named Richard Marques, whose family owned a Deli near

Main and Pitkin Street, took my truck, then fought over it. They were both twice my size even then. When I told Bernard years later, all he wanted to know, was who won. I tried to explain that no one wins in Kindergarten. His sister Rosemarie told me that the family moved from the Bronx, NY to East Hartford for a job at Pratt and Whitney Aircraft in the early '40s.

My folks did the same, as P&W was heavily advertising for help in the New York newspapers. My mother knew their aunt and when I was about nine, she introduced us to Bernard and his older brother Joe at Rockaway Beach, aka, "The Irish Riviera" in Queens, NY, where both our families vacationed. If you lived in New York and were even a little Irish you knew about Rockaway Beach and Rockaway Playland. In many ways it was the Disneyland of our era.

At the Willow, Johnny Hollis was often on the lookout for a boxing match out back in the parking lot. He usually got one and he usually won the match. RIP, Johnny.

Benny Romano would wander into the Willow and say nothing to anyone at least for twenty minutes. We all liked Benny. He was proud and unique, in a fun way, and he always sported the latest men's fashions. I once purchased the same tan suede winter coat from Bassocks and he never let me live it down.

He would be followed by Bob Menger and Billy White, my friend since 5th grade, and who I discuss at length in my book *Whatever Happened to the Pecords?*, available via *www. KeyPublishingCompany.com www.Amazon.com/ books*

Billy and I hung out at King Court, played basketball, and vicious sandlot football games. The fact that there was a good number of pretty girls our age had nothing to do with it. In my Pecords book, I tell the story of how we came close to shooting each other with a 30/30 rifle owned by Roger Borden and his stepbrother. It is a scary story.

When I was at Central, I had the opportunity in '68 to go to Germany over Christmas break: $150 round trip on Lufthansa! I invited Bobby Menger as a guest. I could write a chapter on that trip, but for now, I'll just say that after we landed in Munich, we went straight to bed at a local hotel. We had taken off in the middle of one of the worst snowstorms to ever hit JFK International Airport. I was certain the flight would be canceled. Nope, we took off almost on time. We had the run of the plane and anything we wanted to eat or drink. It was available at no charge.

Because we were up the whole trip flirting with the friendly German Airline Stewardesses, we went to sleep at a Munich Hotel immediately after landing.

I awoke first and went out to find coffee. I noticed the sidewalks were crowded with people carrying skis. After a couple of tries, I was able to question some who could speak English. I found that almost everyone was heading for the German Alps for the New Year's Holiday. I didn't wait to check with Bob, I went into the Bahnhof (railway station) and purchased two tickets. We left by train that morning for Garmisch in the Bavarian Alps. Once there, we stayed in an awesome B&B that reminded me of a Christmas Gingerbread House surrounded by huge mountains covered in snow, owned by the director of the Garmisch Philharmonic, whose daughter looked like a movie star.

We used our military ID's (I was still in the Marine Reserves at the time; Bob was a Navy veteran) to take skiing lessons from veterans of the former German WII Skijaeger Division [First Ski Division]at an American Army Base at the bottom of the Zugspitze, Germany's highest mountain.

After four days, figuring that we were now experts, we hopped on a mountain cog train and skied from the top of Zugspitze to the base of the mountain.

Not saying how many times we fell, but we did it. Bob fell a lot more than me. *Just kidding!*

Maybe just a little more... No, not true. Sorry, Bob.

We also visited a lot of tourist attractions, castles, historic towns and even went to see an International Hockey Game at Innsbruck, Austria which was fairly close by. Russia vs. Germany.

We ended our trip with a visit to the famous Hofbräuhaus in Munich, meeting up with many of the guys from the Veterans Club, drinking beer, and singing songs. There were like 100 long picnic tables in the main hall filled with local Germans and tourists. A couple of things that you couldn't do there were, take one of their famous HB beer mugs, or dance. I wanted a mug, but also knew that some guys got seriously beaten up by the German bouncers outside for trying to abscond with one.

So I asked a German girl to dance and was quickly stopped by guards. That gave me the idea to tick them off by getting up and dancing a second time, with a mug under my trench coat. I was promptly escorted out of the building, trench coat, mug and all. I have it to this day. *Dumb youthful move!* I could have bought one for cheap. I knew that, but I wanted a story behind it. As I said earlier, don't emulate all the stuff I did, especially the dumb stuff! You might think I would have more sense as I was much older than the average college kid. For two dollars, I could have bought a brand new unused mug and avoided possibly getting my nose broken. Dumb, dumb, near-stupid move. Again some unseen force was watching over me.

I learned of this force in 1971. This something or someone prevented a catastrophe, and I am sure many of my generation's Baby Boomers could share similar stories in their own lives. Although they might not want to, and I understand. So that's a brief glimpse of our trip. Germany was never the same. I wanted to pay Bobby back for getting me hired as an on-call beer delivery assistant for the local Budweiser Franchise. I think I did!

The year before, the Travel Manager of the Hartford Triple-A [American Automobile Association] Travel Dept. where I worked weekends and summers, got me 2 tickets on The SS Homeric, sister ship to the famous '60s Oceanic cruise ship, berthed on the Hudson in Manhattan. It was for a seven-day cruise to Paradise Island in the Bahamas. During college spring break. I gave the extra ticket to Billy Carbone and we went on one of the best cruises of our young lives. Like the trip to Germany, I could easily write a chapter or more on that trip. I was always a doer. Not sure where it came from—probably my mother.

Sometimes after playing cards all afternoon at the Willow, we would play late night Setback sessions at John Choquette's house, sometimes coming back in the morning to finish up. His wife was pretty cool about it. We did some crazy stuff.

Big Jim's was another P&W bar we hung out at a little further south on Main Street. "What is it?" the owner, "Big Jim," would always mumble in a "duh nasal" speaking fashion when we came in.

My buddies and I could all imitate his speaking mannerisms. The bar's decor was a little more night clubbish than The Willow and he often had what we called live "Sh*t Kicking music."

Believe it or not, the scene motivated me to somehow graduate college. Big Jim always implored me not to go into his business: the hours, the nights, etc. etc., so I never considered owning a bar or a restaurant. And there weren't many restaurants in town unless you consider the Triple-A Diner one. There were tons of bars and taverns especially in the south end where I lived due to the factory.

Everyone I knew from highschool frequented the Triple-A Diner back then, especially Friday nights after all the clubs emptied, for a late-night breakfast or a turkey club or sometimes just to harass Joannie, the iconic waitress of the decade of the '60s.

Missing a few front teeth, very tall, almost 6 feet and wearing what looked like a white nurse's uniform. She acted like a drill sergeant and she took no sh*t from any of the glossy-eyed patrons. The food was the best, but the place on a Friday night was chaotic and that's an understatement; between Joannie and her waitress colleagues yelling orders, plates crashing, arguments, guys sh*t-faced, and sometimes mini brawls, it was a crazy place. So what was the attraction? Great food and a place to meet. Everybody in our age bracket would eventually show up on a Friday night.

I guess I wasn't the only one who liked the action. It could have been in a movie scene.

Every booth had a jukebox and "Over and Over," Bobby Day, 1958, and later and most popular, the '65 version by the Dave Clark Five seemed to always be the song of choice at one or two a.m.! I can still hear it... "I said over and over again, This dance is gonna be a drag....." followed by Little Bitty Pretty One, also first recorded by Bobby Day, 1957. "Little bitty pretty one, Come on talk-a to me..." This was the way it was every Friday night. Then I would get up Saturday morning and force myself to do two to three hours of homework. Very difficult to do!

I might be working at the Hartford Automobile Club that evening, or possibly third shift. If so, I would be able to do some more homework as there were very few dispatching calls and the place was empty and eerily quiet.

I mentioned previously that I would bring a sleeping bag if I worked the third shift.

In any event, as I started to say, I would get to The Willow around 1:00 pm for an afternoon of Setback. Frank said to Maloney and me, "If you want to make some money, I would get into the Remere Card game over in the corner. They are all feeling no pain so your chance of winning is almost guaranteed."

Well we never played Remere before and in fact, never heard of it. I cannot even locate it now using google. I'm not even sure how to spell it!

Still, considering who we were playing against it should have been a no brainer. An hour later, we had to borrow money from Frank until payday. We lost our shirts. Those guys who probably couldn't walk a straight line didn't lose one hand. Thanks, Frank!

Half the time I could see the guy next to me's cards. All our buddies were laughing at us. It was a Willow Inn story told for years. Unreal. The only story that outdid it was when a bunch of the Willow guys went to the NIT Basketball Tournament in New York. Fortunately, I didn't go, but a lot of bets got placed (In the $THOUSANDS; No kidding!)

It got a little tense when a 6'6" mob enforcer from Hartford showed up at The Willow the following Friday night. I was pretty sure he was "packing." So I stood at the end of the bar getting ready for the worst.

As it turned out, a guy whose name will be left unmentioned and who was friends with one of The Willow Inn boys, meaning he wasn't a Willow regular, had just gotten a job in the midwest.

They all quickly blamed this kid for placing all the bets from the Madison Square Garden, NYC which wasn't entirely true.

Conveniently, no one knew what state or company he was heading to.

I know he didn't come back even for a visit with his folks for a couple of years. I had gone to St. Mary's with him and we were great friends back then. When I transferred to the high school, he went to a seminary in Hartford. I guess he didn't like it. The situation just seemed to fade away. I don't know if any of the debt was ever paid.

I know I'm not saying a lot about my actual

college experience. That's because it was so atypical. I mean I took the required courses plus electives. Usually carrying 15 credits(Five three-credit courses) a semester, I drove to the campus in New Britain every day.

Often I drove back to the Hartford Automobile Club to work as a dispatcher during the evenings. I tried to schedule my classes so I had a couple of days off during the week. These were days I substitute taught or delivered beer. Then I had to do a lot of homework. I mentioned attending some of the Veteran Clubs dances but that was it. I didn't have a lot of dates with college girls.

I wasn't often available due to the aforementioned schedule, plus I had at least three or four years on most of the female students, who were mostly interested in the athletes and fraternity brothers in their age bracket, and rightly so. I met Jan Czaplicki from Bristol on our Germany trip. She was both very attractive and a nice kid. Then I dated Susan Hersey. She was also pretty, and a nice girl. That was about it, over three years of college.

Most of my dating during college was fix-ups by friends' wives or girlfriends. As I said this was not and could not be a typical college experience. I also did something really stupid. I somehow got a student loan from my friends at the Credit Union and bought a used, but gorgeous silver blue with a dark blue convertible top, 1963 Austin Healey 3000 Sports Car. This shrewdly guaranteed that I would work even harder at my part-time jobs.

Sharon always wondered why I was so easy on our kids when they made crazy moves! I loved the car with its unique motoring hum and an overdrive button that gave it a surge forward when switched while producing an awesome continuous droning sound. With the top down it felt like I was in an open cockpit airplane. One great ride!

One of my first problems was that the Auto Club was threatening to fire me due to one of the perks of my job, "free towing." The Healey's carburetors were "open," which, unbelievably allowed rain to get inside, which caused it to stall. I couldn't comprehend this as I knew they were manufactured in England where it seemed to be raining often! So, leaving Central in the rain, it stalled. I would call Hartford Automobile Club and they would tow me into work. New Britain to West Hartford, a pretty long tow. This happened a lot during inclement weather.

I've heard guys say the best day of their life was when they bought their first boat, the next best day is when they sold it. That was me, except it was for the Healey. So I called John over to my parent's house on Colt Street. We spruced it up and this kid came by with cash and bought it.

Other than the carburetors which he didn't seem to worry about, nothing else was wrong.

Of course, I was far from being a mechanic and I was a little worried about what might happen. He took off down Colt toward the entrance ramp to Route 2 toward Hartford. John and I went back into my house.

I don't know why but I turned off the lights and pulled down the shades and proceeded to my rear window. We watched the Healey moving up the ramp. *Bam!* We heard a crash! Then I saw this long object fall out on the pavement. Oh, no! The muffler system just let go, just like that. What were the odds? It had never given me a problem. I pulled down the rest of our window shades and waited with bated breath. A half-hour, then an hour, No phone call. *Whew!*

My Uncle had just passed and I was given his '62 Chevy Impala. I'll leave the comparison of the two cars to the reader's imagination. I'll just say, Ugh!

To my younger readers, I say "Don't do stupid stuff!" Remember, "Experience is a dear school, but fools will learn in no other!" (Ben Franklin) Early on, I said I would share the good and the not so good. I just did.

I'm still driving and the flashbacks keep coming along with the music, so here you go! "They Often Call Me Speedo but my real name is Mr. Earle" (The Cadillacs, 1955).

Thinking of Speedo and The Cadillacs, one Friday evening I was coming around the corner of Colt and Main Street, heading to The Willow and I saw Billy White walking to the front door. He had just bought a new Ford Mustang which he proudly parked out front.

Jimmy Maloney was sitting in the front passenger side. Having a center console was a new thing. The car started to roll backward; apparently, Billy unknowingly left it partially in gear. He yelled to Jim, who lifted his left leg over the console to hit the brake, but inadvertently struck the gas pedal just as Bob Blinn was pulling up to park with Jimmy Jordan as a passenger.

Yep! Jim backed right into him, so Bob backed up. Bill White is now screaming at Jimmy who kept mistakenly punching the gas pedal and ramming Blinn's father's car. I watched in disbelief.

When it was over Blinn said, "For Christ sakes, I thought we were going to get banged down to Pitkin Street." It was like watching a comedy movie. My mouth was wide open along with my eyes. Blinn felt for years that Bill's auto insurance should pay for the damage to his father's car. RIP, Bobby.

Tony Bonelli was a regular at the Willow Inn. Tony was similar to Dave Prince in that he was also fearless. He would fight anyone at the drop of a hat and he did. There are more than a hundred stories on Tony.

One August weekend, Jimmy and I had just got to our second-floor room at the Andrea Hotel on the beach in Misquamicut, RI. Suddenly we heard some commotion in the courtyard below. We looked out in shock as we watched a police officer with his revolver drawn and pointing while yelling at Tony to stop. Tony was on a ledge just outside and next to our window. What the heck?

He didn't stop. Instead, he crashed through our screen. We had to quickly get him out of our room and noticed some girls in the hall were coming in for the night. Couldn't believe they'd let him in their room—and they did not give him up when the police knocked on their door.

The next morning as I was checking out, I heard a woman screaming at the concierge, saying "He was tall with wavy black hair, and he was in my room; as I sat on the toilet I thought I was talking to my husband, and he answered a lot of my questions."

Could it have been Tony? We left promptly. Tony was later ordered by the court to move to California, and that was the last we saw of him. I liked Tony, who grew up with my friend John Choquette.

In some ways, it appears that he was affected by his home life. I guess we all are to some degree.

If you're a young kid reading this and currently experiencing a challenging home life. There is hope. A number of successful people have been in the same situation.

Hopefully, if it gets too stressful, you will reach out to someone—a teacher, an understanding relative, a close friend—to confide in. It's always best to talk things out confidentially. RIP, Tony!

My friends and I hung out at the Blue Sands

right on the ocean during the summer. There were always huge waves crashing underneath the deck. Great bands on the weekends. You could dance, jump in the ocean, and come back and dance some more till one a.m. The music started at one p.m. on Saturdays.

I can still hear the lyrics emanating from inside the dance hall as we pulled up to the parking lot. "Sugar Pie, Honeybunch, You know that I love you..." ("I Can't Help Myself," Four Tops, 1965,).

The place was packed day and night. It was a blast. Later on, we would walk almost directly across the street and check out the band playing at the Neptune, which I appropriately nicknamed "Fight City."

The place had western swinging saloon doors and just like in the old days you might see a guy being thrown out through those doors as you were driving by. It was crazy. We always had four or five of us together so we never got bothered.

Willow Inn, after remodeling. It was a lot rougher looking in our era. "My College Campus"!

My college campus was primarily the Willow Inn. You have to wonder, considering all my jobs, when and how I got homework and studying done. As I stated earlier, I honestly can't recall. I remember my mother putting on a pot of coffee allowing me to pull "all-nighters" studying for exams, in addition to spending hours in the library.

Once in a while, we would join up with another group including Ray Ramsay and Dave Melody. I mentioned Dave singing "Hooka Tooka" earlier, and that my line foreman Roamy was Ray's uncle. Ray obtained a good job and career at HELCO from which he retired.

We would sometimes meet up at Wishes Pub and later the Hose Company in the Burnside Avenue area, sometimes they would bring Steve O'Neil, a tall kid way over 6 feet whose father was an FBI agent. When Melody jumped from his maroon Ford convertible and raised his Stackpole Moore crew neck sweater over his head you knew the action was about to begin.

Chapter XII

The flashbacks of my college years keep showing up!

I have been driving for almost 3 hours—nothing on the radio at the moment. I seem to have lost the oldies station, so the memories of the '60s, just keep coming, in no particular order.

Oops! the station's back! "Here's my story, It's sad but true..." ("Runaround Sue," Dion, 1961).

One Sunday night Maloney and I pulled into Augie & Ray's and noticed Ernie Verdone's brand new—like. forty-eight hours new!—1964 Burgundy Ford Galaxie sedan parked on the right side and backed in under the spotlight affixed to a telephone pole.

Ernie was a tough kid from Glastonbury. He spent two years in the Army stationed in Newfoundland after the thing I mentioned earlier with the Marines. He was on the boxing team the whole time, so if you wouldn't mess with him before, you're not going to mess with him now. Because of the glare, we couldn't tell who was sitting in the car with him. Suddenly there was a thud! A half-full can of beer dropped on his hood. Bobby Cippola thought he had finished his beer, so he tossed it out and up. *Oh, oh!* I can still see the look on Ernie's face. It was flushed red and his eyes tightly squinting when he eased out of his car to survey the dents. Luckily for Cippola he couldn't find one.

Speaking of Bobby Cippola, I had another flashback to '63 and coming home from Misquamicut with Tony Marchese. We were almost at the top of Apple Hill on Old Rt 2 when I spied Henry Lablanc walking around looking dazed (I had gone to St Mary's grammar school with Henry, he was one year ahead of me in high school). He passed away too young. RIP Henry. Then there was Bobby's brand-new Corvette pretty banged up and he was running around doing God knows what. Bobby had a cute sister Lucille Cippola who was very popular in high school and our Class of '62. If we weren't at The Willow, we most likely could be found hanging out at Augie's. I wrote a few more stories about the place in my Pecord's book.

In one of them, I suggested the possibility that a Beach Boys song, "Fun, Fun, Fun till her daddy takes the T Bird away" was written about an East Hartford guy five or six years older than us, initials BC, who used to meet up in Augie's parking lot with a stunning Glastonbury debutant with long black hair, driving a midnight blue T Bird. She came from a wealthy family and the story goes that when the father found out who she was seeing, He was livid and took the T Bird away! (My intention is not to embarrass anyone here, however, I think the guy has passed and I don't remember what happened to the girl.) I believe their romance ended that night at Augie's.

Willie "Dell" Delgazio, a good guy, who was funny without even trying, married another of my St. Mary's classmates, Glady Moore. RIP Glady.

Cliff Newhall we all remember trying to put the fire out in his father's car at the Hartford Drive-In and ended up in Hartford Hospital for a few hours with a burned hand. I'm sure the hospital is still getting over the fact that about twenty of us decided to visit him there, all at once, Crazy! Cliff married Barbara Budarz. RIP, Barbara. I heard later on that he became a successful franchisee of Midas Muffler in the Carolinas. Everyone liked his younger brother Tommy and his friend Brian Menger, a younger brother of Bob.

Wayne Menard, from Brewer Street, showed up at the Willow one day, looking like Tarzan.

I hadn't seen him in a while, he was sporting a good build and looking fit. I remember him and Jimmy Jordan waiting to catch the bus to the south end at Church Corners after St. Mary's CYO, '58, '59. He was around my size at that time.

He must have been pumping some serious iron in addition to working for the MDC. You had to learn the catechism, but the dances afterward were the "catch" for CYO. He also loved a good "Setback" game and so did I.

Later on, like fifty years later, you will read how Wayne helps me out with this book.

Mickey's Drive-In was our alternative to Augie's when we wanted seafood. One Friday night some guys from the North End of Hartford brought over a bare-chested 300-pound-gorilla-looking guy covered with hair throughout his body and stationed him with no shirt, bare chested, between the dirt parking lot and the main entrance.

I guess they wanted everyone to pay him/them homage to pass by. Most turned around and didn't try to go in. We decided to sit and watch from Billy Carbone's white '56 Chevy convertible. My friend Dave Prince pulled in and I told everyone "watch this." Prince, who I described earlier as fearless, got out of his car and walked by the guy, who grunted at him and put out an arm like a giant STOP sign.

He wasn't puny, but this guy was more than twice his size. Prince turns slightly and kicks the guy square in the cojones and doesn't skip a beat as he walks into Mickey's followed by the rest of us. So much for the homage as they dragged their gorilla into a small pickup truck. East Hartford produced some tough guys. [Please read the testimony to that statement at the end of this chapter.]

One Saturday after a two-hour card game, Jimmy Maloney and I went with The Willow Inn owner Frank Benettieri along with Bob Blinn and some others into town. Bob had told Dave Prince that he could use his Triumph motorcycle while we were gone. While waiting at the red light at Church Corners to head north on Main, we turned our heads to the rear to see what the sirens were all about.

Whiz!! Right by us, so fast, almost a blur... Holy Sh*t! It was Prince on Blinn's motorcycle going about 90 mph through the red light with two cop cars trailing right after him. Blinn's mouth just spread wide open; at first, nothing came out, then a loud, "Jesus!! That's my bike! *Goddammit, Prince!"*

Prince was able to maneuver into some neighborhood backyards. Jimmy Jordan was also in the car with us and was the first to quietly mumble "They won't catch him." They didn't!

Jimmy, a handsome kid from the south end who I wrote about earlier and was in the picture at Gerry Ceniglio's wedding, must have taken boxing lessons because he knew how to handle himself with his hands and was a pretty good pool player as well.

These guys were part of what I called my Willow Inn College Campus.

We also had the famous Jimo Zurick who was also a boxer and a tough one. Jimo looked like a Polish prizefighter. You felt protected when going up against our Manchester arch-rivals during the Thanksgiving Day football games with Jimo nearby.

The same goes for Bobby Blinn from South Windsor—I just told you about his motorcycle and Prince. Bob, a natural athlete, was on his way to becoming a professional baseball player, but got cut. I never learned the details. Bob also hung around the Willow Inn. He ended up owning a pub in Enfield. A handsome tough kid who has passed on. RIP, Bob.

Dave Aylmer and his wild temper didn't take any crap. He became an avid runner and when a car almost clipped him and the driver threw him the bird, he ran and caught up with the car at a traffic light and dragged the driver out of his car, and well, that was that.

Note: Dave showed up on the Cape in the summer of '71, while I was building the Ford Diamond Electric Supply and Warehouse. He told me he was quitting his steam fitter trade and planned to open a bicycle shop on the Cape. I have never heard or seen him since.

"East Hartford was one tough town!" I have always said it, and recently an actor in the Apple TV miniseries, "Saving Jacob," said it. I have contacted the show's producers to find out more info. If I hear back, I'll place it at the end or on my book website: *www.KeyPublishingCompany.com*

Sad Note: A classmate and great kid, Johnny Paolino just passed away as this book is being edited. RIP, Johnny. God bless you!

Chapter XIII

More reminiscing on my career as an electric lineman.

I just went by the Hyannis exit on the Mid-Cape Highway and kept an eye out for the next exit, Higgins Crowell Road, which leads to the center of Yarmouth and Rt. 28.

Joe Pierce and I met at Hartford Electric Light and attended lineman school together. I remember thinking Joe looked the part, I mean he was well over six feet, a good-looking, well-built guy. Height helped a lot, as I said earlier you had to often lean way back once one reached the top of the pole to work on connections. I also remember thinking, "What was I doing here, at 5'7"?"

But I was, and as I always managed to, I found a way to do the job. I've stated before that it was the best blue-collar job and company in the US during the era. The pay was great. In addition, hazardous duty pay was given during storms, plus weekend on-call pay. We didn't have deductibles; our insurance covered everything.

The company provided weekly parties, bands, libations for all. Unbelievable! Night school was 100% paid for regardless of what you got for a grade. The guys were great, everyone could have been my best friend, but you wouldn't mess with any of them—they were all tough guys. When starting out I incorrectly installed a meter for a new home construction site and electrocuted the senior linesman, who looked like John Wayne. I'm not sure, but I think his name was Budrig. I was having a problem installing a meter on the construction meter pole. The shock was due in part to some wet muddy holes surrounding the meter pole.

Hey, no one told me that in some areas like Unionville, CT, the ground (neutral) wire which almost always is the middle wire of the three secondary wires (wires that feed into your house at 115 to 220 volt) was on the bottom, instead of the middle!

When the senior lineman came down off the pole, muttering about these F'*@*# new guys, to help me plug in the meter, cursing all the way, he finally jammed it in, never considering because of the peculiar positioning of the secondary wires that the meter was now "hot."

With one shoe in a puddle, the shock threw him backward about five feet.

I took a lot of grief for my part, but that was it, he never spoke of it again. That's the way it was. A lot different from the corporate life I would later experience.

My East Hartford friend Freddy Henson, recently discharged from the Marines, also a new C Lineman, got into a shouting match with his foreman and ended up throwing a wrench at him. The situation was settled on the spot. Never spoken of again. Try that today!

There was also lots of horsing around. On one of my first climbs, I was helping a senior lineman, Jim O'Neil, a real jokester. I was manually drilling holes at the top of a forty foot pole to install a transformer (sounds easy, but it wasn't), Jim, on the other side, was hoisting up some equipment.

When it was time for lunch, Jim went down first, but for some reason, I couldn't budge; my belt was stuck. Turns out Jim had nailed my belt to the pole. The whole crew stood below laughing their sides off as I dangled forty feet off the ground. That's the way it was!

My decision to leave was gradual and had to do with a severe illness I contracted, Epstein Barr, which lasted four months, and an unfortunate accident that caused the death of one of our roving foremen as I described in the earlier flashback.

He was checking on various crews toward the end of the day when arriving at a job where we had begun hanging replacement wire. He signaled it was time to pack up and head back into our base facility. As a friendly but unnecessary gesture, he got out of his truck and began to pull up the six-foot ground pole attached to the wire spool.

Out of nowhere, a gust of wind a quarter mile down the road hit the loose dead wire that was hanging in loops from large pulleys on each pole awaiting to be connected and pushed it up against a 13,000-volt line, killing him instantly. He had a young family, as he married later in life and was ready to retire in a few months. This horrific death affected everyone and was a reminder of how dangerous this work could be. It also caused me to think that *as great of a job it was, what if physically I could no longer do it, what would I do?*

It was one of my most difficult decisions to leave and go to college full time at twenty-two, especially considering that I didn't like school. "HELCO" was such a great place to work in those days. Of course, you need some big cojones to do that high paying job. Climbing forty-foot poles, handling live wires (one mistake could be your last) is not everyone's cup of tea.

I was reminded of the danger each evening as we showered to go home and noticed some of what appeared to be large wounds on the bodies of fellow linemen which resembled bulky hamburger patties.

They were the exit wounds caused by bumping up against a live wire. I was told they never really healed.

Chapter XIV

"The Greatest..." story begins. I meet the Greatest!

It was 8:00 p.m., and beginning to get dark when I arrived at the cottage on Higgins Crowell Road, Yarmouth, Massachusetts (Cape Cod). I can't recall the address, but I knew it was on the left, midway between the Mid Cape Highway and Rt. 28 (heading west, Rt. 28 would take you to downtown Hyannis). I remember Joe Pierce telling me to look for a Nursery school sign on the left side of the road. Joe and another HELCO employee, Kenny Rasmussen, had rented out the left side of a kids' nursery school for the summer. I know it doesn't sound like much, but it was a cool spot.

The cottage was very rustic in and out with a large stone fireplace. It reminded me of the cabins I had seen in Vermont and the price was right, i.e. "help with the groceries." They got a great deal due to its connection to a nursery school, however, they were mostly there on weekends when the nursery was closed. During the week, it was all mine.

I went to the back door and lifted the mat. No key. I was assured it would be there. Now what? I tried the windows. All were locked!

103

The sun had set and it was getting dark quickly. I had to act, so I broke the back door window and let myself in. Possibly due to my Marine Corps training at Parris Island, I had a "Stay in shape mentality" embedded in my brain. I found a bed and a clock which I set for 6:00 am and immediately fell into a deep sleep. Morning came quickly, and I awoke before the alarm and put on some shorts and sneakers and headed out the door.

The sky was beginning to lighten up and the air was breezy, perfect for a good run. I had gotten about a half mile from the cottage when I came upon a group of black men wearing brightly decorated island shirts.

They were jogging very slowly and blocking the running path. I had to slow down or move into the road. My problem was that the road was already crowded with tourists and vacationers. I caught up with the entourage and asked one of the guys, "What was going on?"

The group were in a circle now and watching someone in the middle who seemed to be bobbing and weaving. At the same time, he also seemed to be clowning around. The guy said, "Aw, he's just fooling around." I said, "Who's he?" "The Greatest," says he. "The Greatest?" I asked. "Muhammed, Muhammad Ali!" he stammered. *Holy sh*t*, I don't think I missed any of his fights. The greatest boxer of all time.

What's he doing on the Cape? "What's it look

like? He's getting into shape for his upcoming fight." Right. I'm thinking I'm being played. He hasn't been in the ring in over three years. I said that the newspapers had reported he was banned from the ring in every state. (This was punishment for refusing to be drafted as he was against the Vietnam War.)

As I gained rapport with this member of his entourage, I was told that while he was banned by the boxing commission of each state, one state, Georgia, didn't have a boxing commission. As it turns out, Ali was friends with Georgia State Senator Leroy R. Johnson, the first African-American to be elected to the legislature in fifty years, and, as an attorney, Leroy knew how to set up the fight.

Thus he was assured if he were to agree to a match, it would be held in Atlanta. I pressed him as to who he might fight. He replied without hesitation, Jerry Quarry. I admit I was skeptical, I mean even if this stuff about Atlanta allowing him to fight were true, he hadn't fought in over forty months. I needed to do some research on Jerry Quarry, who was from California. I didn't know anything about him. Just then, Ali came towards me doing some light jabs.

He had that familiar grin on his face and as I said Hello, he gently tapped my chin with a short jab. I gave him a thumbs up and said I'll be at the fight. I mean I didn't know what to say. Of course, I had no idea how I would get to Atlanta. He said he was impressed that I was out running in the early morning and invited me to join his entourage. I was numb! I thanked him, wished him luck in the upcoming fight, and reiterated that I would get to see it.

Then I just did an about-face and jogged back to the cottage. Stunned, to say the least!

I have regretted not joining him for the rest of his workout ever since.

Meanwhile The Wah-Watusi by The Orlons was playing on the cabin radio. "Come on, take a chance! ... It's the dance made for romance!"

Chapter XV

Half-ass carpenter and the
Witness Protection Program

I wasn't in the cabin for more than a few minutes when I heard a knock on the door. Oh, oh I thought, did someone see me break in and call the police.

I tepidly opened the door thinking the worst. I stared at an older rugged-looking guy, unshaven, with white and gray hair. He bluntly said, "I saw you running this morning." Yeah? What about it?" said I.

"Well, I have a contract to build a two-story electric supply and warehouse across the street. You want a job?" *Sure*, said I. "Great! My name is Spike (name changed for this story), and I need one more guy, but you can start tomorrow morning." As mentioned, I needed some R&R... but I also needed money.

As it turned out, since I had to attend summer school, all of the bartending jobs were taken earlier by other college kids who finished school in May. Plus, I thought it could certainly be more convenient working right across the street.

Whatever! It might be my only choice. Spike left and I turned to make some coffee. I was feeling overwhelmed, in a good way. I met the greatest boxer of all time and I landed a summer job!

Spike said "If anyone asks what you're doing, just tell 'em you're a half-ass carpenter." He also assured me that he would teach me all that I needed to do. Hopefully you, my readers, are getting the perspective of my first book's title *Jump In and Start Swimming!*

I have to admit the first two weeks on the job were brutal. I was using muscles that I didn't know I had, and it was hot. In the beginning, it was mostly bull work, including moving, carrying wood, and bringing building supplies. The temperature remained in the high eighties every day and there was no shade, as we hadn't put a roof on yet. Soon we started building, and my right arm muscles ached from eight to nine hours of pounding nails. Slowly, each day, my body began to get acclimated to my newfound construction job.

I often arrived an hour early and stayed an hour later, averaging approximately ten hours per day, plus some half day Saturdays. I was paid a little more than minimum wage and they didn't take out taxes, so I guess I was considered a contract employee. I opened an --account with the Cape Cod Bank on Rt. 28, near the Yarmouth Police Station. Every Friday, I cashed my check, keeping just enough to buy groceries and have some fun at the Velvet Hammer Night Club in downtown Hyannis, while depositing the rest in the bank.

One of my extra duties was to make a coffee run each morning into Yarmouth, for which I usually borrowed Joe Pierce's 750 Triumph Motorcycle, not a Harley, but a big bike.

This worked until, one morning as I rounded a back road off Higgins Crowell—a shortcut to avoid tourist traffic—I hit some sand and the rear tire of the bike started to skid. Luckily, I had the good sense and reflexes to dive off and roll in a grassy knoll on the side of the road. I can still see the horrified look on the faces of the tourists stopped at the traffic light. Fortunately, I only received a few scratches—however, the Triumph didn't do as well. I began taking my car for coffee: One doesn't often get a second chance with a motorcycle. Plus, I never got a license.

I never asked Spike why he had a California license plate. I mean he had a thick Massachusetts accent and I thought I heard him say he was from Leominster, MA. One day we had an extra kid on the job. His name was Billy. Billy, a tough city kid, said his girlfriend was Al's 19-year-old gorgeous daughter. He was down from Somerville, Mass. for a couple of weeks to visit and Spike offered him a job.

Billy happened to overhear me mentioning Spike's California license plate and began telling me and the other college kid, Jake, one of the wildest stories that I ever heard. First, he told us that Spike and his family were in the Witness Protection Program and were relocated to California.

Our eyes began to widen as he continued to say, "It wasn't because of Spike!." I knew that Spike was part of an infamous family, Leominster Ironworkers, the Bissells (name and other information changed), who hung around the Combat Zone, a now-closed section of Boston that was home to strip clubs, rowdy bars, and many brawls. It was eventually shut down in 1993, after a college kid got stabbed in front of one of the bars.

We were stunned, Billy continued telling us that Spike's son Rob was home alone in their Leominster apartment on his 21st birthday. His parents found out that morning that they had to attend a wake for a relative in Springfield, leaving Rob alone on his big day.

Rob decided to go down the block from the family apartment to get his first beer. Upon entering the local pub, he realized he was alone with the owner who bought him a draft and went into the back room. The phone began ringing and the owner shouted out for Rob to answer. Someone was looking for his girlfriend named Shelly.

Rob politely told the caller that she was not there. and hung up. The phone rang again and the caller insisted that he be allowed to speak with Shelly. Rob again said she wasn't there and that the owner said she had not been all there that day. The calls kept coming and coming until finally, Rob told the caller to f. off, as he slammed the phone down.

Rob began to enjoy his first beer.

Approximately twenty minutes elapsed since the last call. As he took a sip he couldn't help noticing in the bar's mirror that he was facing, that the door behind him was slowly opening.

There was, as he later would describe, a big goon standing there looking quite disheveled. The goon proceeded to walk slowly over to him and simultaneously grabbed his belt and the top of his shirt collar. And threw him across the bar face-first into the mirror and bottles.

Rob lay there bleeding and dazed for a couple of minutes. When he got up on his hands and knees and started to crawl out, he was able to turn his head slightly and watched his assailant take his old seat and began nonchalantly finishing off his beer. Rob made it back to the family apartment and was both shocked and angry to see his face in the bathroom mirror. He looked like he had just run through thirty feet of thorn and pricker bushes. Without bothering to even wipe his face, he moved quickly into his parent's bedroom. Locating a key to one of the smaller closets, he retrieved a rifle in which he loaded with some bullets. He walked down the steps out into the street and made it as quickly as he could to the bar. He swung the door open, took aim at the goon, and pulled the trigger. Wham! He watched as the guy fell off the barstool and left as he heard a clunk. All our eyes were popping out of their sockets. as we listened to this crazy wild tale.

Billy continued his story, "By 4:30 the next morning, the Bissell family were all on an American Airlines flight to California. The goon was a high up member of a mob family."

Visiting with relatives had to be done under the cloak of darkness.

The best way to travel, although a grueling trip, was by car, and the Cape allowed relatives from Leominster to reunite in a relatively short time. The Bissells weren't rich, so Spike had to secure an income while being on vacation. That was one thing he and I had in common: We were workers.

Growing up in Connecticut, we heard very little about the mob. It was there, no doubt, but it was not until the early seventies that the newspapers started publishing stories of a mob guy being arrested or someone being shot in a mob-related incident.

Later on, I would read the book *Squeal,* by the famous crime reporter, Les Coleman. Les, with the help of a snitch, tells the story of how the mob began and grew in Hartford, CT. and the surrounding area.

I have never tried to prove that the Bissell story was true or made up. I just assumed it was true. I will tell you though, that after Billy's story, I kept a watchful eye on the continuous traffic on Higgins Crowell Road!

The thought that someone could come down

from Boston and "take out" Spike at this site kept creeping into my mind. *Note: I had to change all the names and personal information in this tale to protect those still living.*

Lunchtime and The Morse Code of Love, by The Capris, is blaring from our transistor radio. "I sent my baby a telegram asking to be her dit dot man…"

I think I mentioned that Spike didn't drink alcohol which I thought was odd due to his toughness and previous line of work. Tough? I watched a plank on some metal staging suddenly spring up and smack him square in the face.

It would have leveled most guys. He never cried out. He wiped away the blood with his hand and kept hammering. Ouch!

As I said, the Bissells were said to hang out in the Combat Zone after work. To this day I don't trust guys who never take a drink or those who smoke a pipe. Not sure why, I just never did. Having said that I did trust Spike, mostly. As I grew older I realized the amount of courage and will power that guys often had to muster to quit and save their lives. Isnt that what life is about—learning?

Three weeks into the job, I realized that Spike did have a vice. He announced on a Friday morning that we were due for some R&R, so he proposed we all take a ride with him to some park. Naively, I never heard of Rockingham Park. I was from Connecticut. A park was a park! I assumed it was an amusement park, but, to my surprise, this was a horse race track. I should mention that this particular morning Spike hung onto our paychecks. Well, within a few hours Spike went through his paycheck, mine, Billy's, and Jake's. His son Rob wasn't at work that morning. Quite frankly, he showed up infrequently.

As I mentioned, his brother-in-law John, who looked like he was in the mob, worked with us part-time. Spike cashed his paycheck as well. Not good!

I agreed to work Saturday morning. Still bristling at the fact that I let a week's paycheck disappear at Rockingham, I felt I needed to make up for it, so I showed up Saturday. John, Spike's brother in law, showed up (he usually worked a half day on Saturdays). John was rugged looking. I wouldn't want to mess with him.

He also liked Yours Truly a lot; not sure why. Maybe because I minded my own business, never took a day off, worked hard, and got along with everyone. The owner of the Ford Diamond Electric, Joe Ford, would also show up every Saturday.

I put my carpenter's belt on, said Hello, and waited for the fireworks. I kept my distance, but I could hear the yelling and cussing. There were a couple of shoves, but that's as far as things got. *Whew!*

A week later, John and his wife invited all of us to be their guest at a family-style Italian restaurant on the outskirts of Hyannis. Spike and his wife came and everything seemed "hunky-dory." I never went to Rockingham again that summer. I did notice Joe Ford showing up Friday evenings and personally began handing out our checks. Hmm!

In researching Spike for this story, I located a journal some family members wrote about the Bissels that included Spike's early years and marriage in the 1940s. I am hesitant for obvious reasons to publicize it, although it was put up on the internet. It mentions Spike's fondness for the track.

The following excerpt from the journal was an *"ah-ha!"* moment for me: "Shortly after he got married, his sister-in-law came by for a visit. She asked his wife (name redacted) where the silverware set was that she had given them as a wedding present. Spike's wife was confused and as Spike walked in she confronted him. The tale goes on to say that, "he ran down the hallway to their bedroom and locked himself in."

Later, the journal stated that he came out and confessed that he took the set, sold it, and went to the track. I was floored. I had seen alcoholics on TV, and also drug addicts, but I had never seen a gambling addict until that afternoon in Rockingham. The look on his face was identical to the look on other addicts I had seen after a binge, disheveled, nervous. *Note: All of the names etc. in this story had to be changed for their protection. I do have the journal and maybe at some point I can show it on my book website www. KeyPublishingCompany.com.*

Chapter XVI

Hippie beads and brawl at the Velvet Hammer.

The construction site was being transformed and as I left each evening and crossed the street to the cabin. Remember Joe Pierce's cabin was located on Higgins Crowell Road—talk about convenient! I could see an actual building beginning to form as the result of all our hammering. It felt good. And my bank account was growing and that made it feel even better. A pair of cutoffs was my only uniform and my hair which was a Marine Corp buzz cut through '69, now curled up in the back of my neck.

Carloads of girls on their way to Hyannis for vacation would honk and wave and sometimes stop for directions. Most likely because Jake looked like Adonis: blonde, great build, and handsome.

We were always on the second floor or roof at this point. Some girls placed what I called hippie beads around my neck. There is a picture somewhere. Oops there *was*—my wife Sharon tore it up! Jake got the dates and I got the beads. Those beads ended up causing me some problems.

My roommates, Joe Pierce and Kenny

117

Rasmussen, and I, usually ended up at the Velvet Hammer, in downtown Hyannis, most Friday nights.

This one Friday however, both had been delayed in Connecticut, so I ended up going by myself, with plans for us to meet up later in the evening.

The Velvet Hammer had the best bands and was considered one of the best nightclubs in Hyannis. When I arrived the band was playing "Chicago" which debuted in April '69 by The Chicago Transit Authority. I remember thinking, what a great band the Velvet Hammer had that summer! The place was packed. After all, it was the middle of July and the Cape was a major vacation destination in the Northeast. For Boston, it was "thee" place for a Friday night, a weekend, or longer.

I noticed the girls who gave me the beads earlier in the day, standing by the bar. There were two big guys wearing construction boots and clothes trying to engage them in a conversation. One of the girls waved to me and I waved back as I headed into the men's room. As I started to make my way back to the main seating area of the club, one of the construction guys, obviously drunk, was singing—if you could call it that—an Irish song, and blocking my return entrance.

The guy was huge; there was no way to get by. He said he liked my beads as he reached for them and I tried to defuse the situation and said "I like

Irish music."

To which he snidely replied "No kidding," as he twisted the beads in his fist, choking me in the process. He then said in a garbled Boston accent, "Well lets you and I go out back and do some singing." *Oh sh*t,* I thought.

This is not a good situation. Without a thought, I slapped his hand down and moved quickly around him. He followed, I went down the closest aisle between tables, noting that the band and its stage was the last stop. He kept following.

Either I would have to jump on the stage and run through the band members and their instruments or... what? The "what" was a wall at the end! I was hurrying down the aisle, and from the corner of my eye I could see him moving and kicking chairs out of the way.

"For Christ's sake, he just pushed a waitress on top of a table." "The jerk is out of control!" Of course, this is all happening at lightning speed. I didn't have time to imagine what all the touristy guests were thinking. Probably that I was about to get killed. I suddenly stopped, turned to face him, and tried to appear like I was looking behind him and I yelled *POLICE!!*

He turned slightly, and as he did I swung upward, lifting my whole body into it, and nailed his nose. Note that this was after three weeks, ten hours a day, pounding nails!

As they say, "the bigger they are the harder

they fall," and he dropped on his back while I followed on top of him swinging repeatedly at that already broken nose. In seconds, the bouncers had me and him. I said "Hey! He attacked me and my fiancée" and beckoned to the startled girl who had earlier given me the beads. Fortunately, she went along.

I remember a stranger came up as I was escorted out and said "That was the best punch I've ever seen!" Of course, no one made any attempt to help me. In fairness, patrons were in total shock. This wasn't some seedy gin mill. When they brought us—meaning me and my supposed fiancée—onto the front steps, the police had the guy up against a car, and were going through his wallet as he was still bleeding profusely. I later heard he spent the night in the Hyannis jail. Thankfully I never saw him again!

The young girl disappeared in the crowd probably in disbelief of what she just witnessed. I didn't blame her! My roommates finally showed up, and I noticed that one of the bouncers was Scottie Pettie, a friend of all of us. Scottie, as it turned out, served in the Air Force with my neighborhood friend Ugo Beneteiri, while stationed near Bangor, Maine. It's a small world. *Coincidence?* I'm sure Scottie helped prevent me from getting arrested.

Saturday morning I showed up at 8:00 a.m., and planned on working until noon. Spike yelled over, "Hey Muhammed! I hear you have a great right hook."

News travels quickly on the Cape. Spike was tied in here, in Yarmouth and Hyannis. Nothing got by him.

You could tell he was proud that his "half-ass carpenter" was able to take care of himself. I wasn't a fighter by nature, but growing up in the blue-collar town of East Hartford, I learned how to defend myself after having the sh*t kicked out of me several times. It came in handy a few times that summer on the Cape, as well.

Jake, the other college kid on our team, managed to borrow a small sailboat that we would launch from Centerville Beach and head toward the Vineyard, often on Saturdays after we put in four hours at the building.

We did this sailing routine for a couple of weeks. On this one clear, sunny Saturday, about midway between Centerville Beach and the Vineyard, we began heading back in. I was in the rear, manning the rudder and Jake was adjusting the sail. The bow began lifting out of the water as if a huge wave was rolling beneath us.

However, there weren't any waves and the water was as calm as I had seen it in the last few weeks. Looking down to my left, I could see a shadow passing from underneath the boat which looked like a small submarine. Jake saw it too and yelled "What the hell was that?"

On Monday the *Cape Cod Times* ran a story and a photo of a Great White Shark basking off the coast of Martha's Vineyard. It was about five feet longer than our sailboat.

The story went on to describe that several great white sharks have been "summering" off the coast since May. We quickly switched to surfing (learning how) up at Nauset Beach. As I'm writing, I'm hearing that Nauset now has a Great White Shark problem.

The Ford Diamond Electric Supply Corp. was taking shape. Joe and Kenny had a bunch of friends from Hartford, and were continuously hosting parties. It seemed that people were coming and going from the cabin all day long. If we were not at the Velvet Hammer, we were in Falmouth Heights at the famous Casino by The Sea. The Cape was a fun place to be in the summer of 1970. Seemed that everyone at the cottage could cook except for me. Joe Pierce would often say, "Naughton, what do you think? I'm your mother?"

Did I build this? No way! Yes, I did!
Summer of 1970, I was a "half-ass carpenter"
—and IT'S STILL STANDING!—on Higgins
Crowell Road, Yarmouth, Massachusetts.

Chapter XVII

The Summer fun continues: the casino by the sea,
Falmouth Heights, Sonny's of Falmouth, and Zack's!

Sunday afternoons, we were at the famous Casino By The Sea on the ocean in Falmouth Heights. It was always jam-packed. A fun place to hang out. Saturday nights, we would go to a club in Falmouth called "Sonny's," located just at the beginning of the town and near the bus depot on the road leading to Woods Hole, where you could catch the ferry to Martha's Vineyard.

Sonny's had the best oldie bands from Boston. They always played a few Irish Rebel songs and ended the night with patriotic music with a rock & roll beat. Occasionally we would head over to Zacks, a large nightclub on the outskirts of Falmouth. Zacks also had the best end-of-the-season St Patrick's Day Party. There would be hundreds of guys and gals, now Baby Boomers, attending. This was a fabulous time to be young and single at the Cape. You always had the sweet smell of the surrounding ocean and you could often hear the music booming from the clubs as you drove by. Everyone seemed happy and all with the same goal: "Just have a good time."

Here's the thing: That summer, the Vietnam War was raging, South Vietnam forces attacked Cambodia, and I mentioned earlier that four student protesters were shot and killed in May at Kent State. As I wrote earlier, fifty thousand American boys, average age nineteen, died.

As I think back to that year, as long as you didn't have a brother or other relative over there, you, at least those of you in your mid-twenties, hardly gave it a thought. It was pretty much "where is the next party?" Nope, *life is not always fair.*

God forgive us! Young fellow Americans were dying in the jungle, nine thousand miles away. As a former Marine, I'm embarrassed to admit it took till April 1992, when we stopped in DC on the way home from our Spring Break family trip to Disney and visited "The Wall," to be fully impacted.

With my wife and kids, we watched gray-haired parents searching, copying and crying. Seeing all the thousands of names on the Wall left us speechless and thinking, *My God! What have we done?* I tried several times during the rest of the way home, to answer the questions of my sons Timmy, 17, Matt, 15, and daughter Erin, 14, about The Wall and the war. I was not successful. Eight brave women nurses also died in that war.

Chapter XVIII

"I might have saved his life!"
Attacked leaving Sonny's of Falmouth.

One Saturday, a friend of Joe Pierce's whose first name was George fixed me up with his fiancée's girlfriend. Up until recently, I couldn't remember his last name nor my date's name. I did recall that he worked for the MDC, which provides water in the Hartford area. I also remember that he said he hung out at the Rocking Horse Restaurant in the south end of Hartford. He then proceeded to tell me that he worked with Wayne Menard, a friend of mine that I mentioned earlier from East Hartford. Maybe it didn't matter, except to me, but I could not recall his last name as I hoped to speak to him before this got published. I contacted the MDC and they were surprisingly helpful. A long-time human resource employee remembered two Georges: One ended up becoming president of the MDC, and both were about my age. The HR employee said they both had died.

I described Wayne earlier in my book. In any event, I mention George here, because I might have saved his life outside the nightclub Sonny's in Falmouth. George and his fiancée (I think

125

her name was Nancy), an Italian blonde with a Scandinavian look, and her girlfriend whose name I said I can't recall, and Yours Truly, headed out in two cars to Sonny's.

The band, as expected, was terrific, and we danced almost till closing. We had parked our cars in a parking lot out in the back of Sonny's, near the bus depot. We began walking up the incline toward the lot on Depot Road where tourist buses also parked. Suddenly we heard a loud belligerent noise coming up behind us. I noted that it was coming from six or seven huge guys who had been causing trouble inside at the bar.

I slightly turned my head and told George and his girlfriend, who were directly behind us to begin walking faster. Their slurred speaking suggested that they were from some fraternity associated with a Massachusetts college football team. As I said, they were huge. I could sense them purposely swearing and getting closer.

What happened next was a little chaotic. One of the guys pulled George around by his shoulder and took a swing at him. *Sh*t*, I thought. My instant instinct was to start a commotion to try to get their attention. I jumped onto the middle of the street which by this time was crowded with cars exiting the clubs, hoping to attract a cop, anybody.

I started yelling obscenities at the group, calling them college f*rts, and began challenging them. I hoped if they got me, someone would jump in or a cop would hear me. At that point I didn't

care if I got arrested. Again, my main purpose
was to give George and his fiancée and my date
a chance to escape. I then saw that two guys
had pinned each of Georges's arms against the
wrought iron fence, allowing their buddies to take
sucker punches at him.

This was happening fast, in seconds. I noticed
one of the punks began taking running swings
at him, actually coming into the street running
around a parked car and sucker punching him in
the face, so my plan wasn't working. The guy was
tall and slender, around 5'11". I crouched out of
sight by the car and swung upward as he was in
stride, heading for George a second time. I nailed
his chin with an uppercut, and he seemed to level
out in the air before falling to the pavement. I
screamed for them to look at their fallen asshole
buddy. I got their attention! The chase was on.
Down the street I ran.

Away from the bus depot toward the bottom of
Depot Road, I wove in and out of cars stuck in the
after-hours traffic with the jerks in pursuit yelling
"Let's kill the bastard!" across Locust Street, and
into the Hunt Club. Hopefully, George and the girls
escaped. The Hunt Club was packed. I crashed
through the mob.

Every guy had a blazer or military dress
uniform except for me. The girls looked like
debutants. Without a moment's hesitation, I
barged into the men's room. Locking the door, I
saw a reasonably sized window that I opened. The
banging on the door felt like it would burst open

any second. Instinctively, I jumped through and kept going. I found a coffee shop up on Palmer Street and waited there for about an hour.

I had to get back up the hill to the desolate parking lot to retrieve my car. Would they be there waiting for me? Nope, mine was the only car left, and no sign of anyone.

I was lucky the football players were drunk and the bathroom in the Hunt club had a decent size window. Also, the carpentry work had gotten me into great shape. I never saw George or his finance or my date again. Years later, someone told me they got married.

As I said earlier, I was not a fighter per se but, after growing up in East Hartford, I watched a bunch, and learned from them. Of course, after getting my butt kicked several times, I eventually learned how to use defensive moves, many I had learned at Parris Island. Running, if necessary, could be one of them.

Coincidentally—by now you know my feelings on coincidences—after fifty plus years, I recently reunited with Sheila Condon via LinkedIn, a type of business Facebook. She just happened across my name and remembered me from St. Mary's sixty years ago; I mean of all times? I have been on LinkedIn due to my books for over twelve years. Why now? Sheila and I were classmates at St. Mary's elementary school. I recall her as a mature, sweet, and a nice, pretty kid. Our connection was just happenstance. Or was it?

We got into a discussion initially via LinkedIn and told her about my story, "The Greatest," that I was writing, and my search for a man named George who worked for the MDC. As it turned out, she had grown up with Wayne Menard's wife, Rosemary. You might recall at the beginning of this book I mentioned Wayne and a bunch of us who played "Setback" at The Willow Inn.

When I told Sheila more about this story I was writing, she contacted her friend Rosemary, and within a few hours, I had a long telephone conversation with Wayne, who confirmed that he worked with George Mercadante at the Hartford MDC back in the day.

So in the first five minutes of our phone call, I now had George's last name. Unbelievable! He also confirmed that George passed away in 2011. I then unsuccessfully tried to contact George's wife Nancy. I think it was fifty years ago when I last spoke with Wayne. As I have said, when I meet up or speak to East Hartford friends, it's like I last saw them a week ago.

Again, what were the chances I would get a request from Sheila to connect on LinkedIn after so many years? And what were the odds she was childhood friends with Wayne's wife Rosemary? I still say there is no such thing as a coincidence, but what is it? Maybe the whole situation with George and his fiancée was blown out of proportion. Maybe they didn't think I saved his/their lives. Maybe the whole scene was perceived as an embarrassment to George?

Maybe they thought I was the cause of the altercation and that I just ran away. I don't know, *maybe I think too much!*

Remember me telling you about my crazy college campus, the Willow Inn? And the related tough guy stories? Well, Wayne's sons became extremely successful: One is an engineering supervisor for the utility company, Eversource that acquired HELCO, where I once worked as an apprentice lineman!

His other son is a principal in one of East Hartford's Schools. My kids, along with most of those other guys, also went on to be successful. What's the point? I'm not 100% sure, except we must have had something special that we didn't know about in the early days. Something we passed on. And for my part, I didn't want my kids doing some crazy stuff that I had done. Typical father.

Chapter XIX

More building, job fairs, and learning to use my mind.

For most of August, I continued to work ten hours a day, plus Saturday morning. We pretty much built everything, including the roof trusses. I guess that purchasing them pre-assembled was too expensive. I didn't care what we did. I just kept shoving 70% of my "under the table pay" into the bank at the end of the week. Our partying usually began on Fridays and lasted through Sunday night, unless my roommates took vacation time. In that event, we could be partying for a week straight. Whatever beer I drank seemed to sweat out of my body in the heat of the day.

I received word from my friend and fellow graduate John Choquette that the job market back home was heating up, albeit slowly. No, I never gave much thought about the opportunities that were opening up right on the Cape. I could have probably bought an inexpensive piece of land and built a house, got my real estate license and created a money-making real estate company.

I guess I was just so brainwashed, having

grown up in my early years in a project and watching my parents go to work each day in a factory, I believed I needed to get a white-collar job. I also realize that I could have applied to Pratt & Whitney, but I wanted something different.

For me, white-collar symbolized higher pay. Plus, I probably would never have met my wife Sharon (Sharon Maureen McCarthy) and have the beautiful family I have been blessed with. Who knows? Maybe heaven would have directed her to the Cape for vacation, and we would have met at the Velvet Hammer. Probably not, as she didn't go to clubs.

So I went back to a Job Fair in Hartford, then another, and another. In September, I stopped by a table manned by employees of The Travelers Insurance Company. As I was grabbing a brochure, a man said Hello, and we began talking. He said his name was Wayne Wall, and he was the Hartford District Group Insurance Manager. I told him my childhood friend, Jim Maloney, worked for The Travelers.

Wayne excitedly said, "I know: I hired him!" He then suggested I meet him at his office the following week. I wasn't sure. I didn't want to jump on my friend Jim's train so to speak. At the same time, I was out of school for three months, and my folks were beginning to put some pressure on me as to why I didn't already have a job.

Someone left a book *There Is A River,* by Edgar Cayce, the most gifted psychic of the 20th century, on the coffee table at our cabin. We had loads of people, friends of friends, stopping by often throughout the summer and often forgetting personal items. This was an unusual item. I picked it up and couldn't put it down. It is an incredible life story of an ordinary man who could predict the future, and locate oil beneath the ground. He predicted the discovery of Aspirin and offered healing herbal concoctions still in existence, and used to this day.

It got me thinking "outside the box." After finishing the book I had a stranger walk up to me in the Cape Cod Mall and hand me an audiotape. The tape was "The Strangest Secret," by Earl Nightingale. Nightingale offered another "think outside the box" message. His message is the theory and the belief that "we become what we think about." I had discovered these theories at least once before, so I recognized that someone, something, some unseen force, was suggesting I read them once again. I listened, read and began to employ these messages in my own life. I had never seen that stranger before.

Soon after I noticed a book on display at the Hyannis Mall bookstore, *Psycho-Cybernetics,* by Dr. Maxwell Maltz. Dr. Maltz was a cosmetic surgeon who began to investigate why many of his patients kept on seeing themselves as they were before the surgery. This led to many discoveries regarding the power of the subconscious mind. There was a story in the book about an Army Major who was imprisoned for five years at the Hanoi Hilton during the Vietnam war.

While in his small prison cell he played a round of golf in his mind every day. He said he imagined and felt the grass, the club, and the ball. When finally released, he entered and won a golf tournament in Atlanta.

He hadn't played except mentally for six years! Another story told of two finalists in the English dart-throwing championship. To prepare, one of them went into a pub in London and threw darts for hours each day.

The other rented a cabin in the Scottish highlands and hung a large white sheet over the living room wall. He would sit for hours imagining a dartboard and feel himself throwing bulls eyes during the day. Who won? The latter finalist, who used his mind. The book contains many similar stories depicting the power of the mind, which began to resonate with me.

As Earl Nightingale suggested, I wrote my goal on a piece of paper and put it in my car's glove compartment (I didn't have a lot of privacy in our cabin at the time). I was baptized Catholic and attended Catholic School through ninth grade, so I always prayed in addition to employing the theories regarding the subconscious. For me, they went hand in hand.

I wrote a very simple statement, "I will find a career." For me, that meant wearing a white shirt and tie.

As I stated before I went back to school out of fear of possibly not being able to continue as a lineman due to health or injury.

I thought that I might want to be a high school teacher, however, after substitute teaching for three years, I decided that while I enjoyed it, I didn't want to do it for a career.

I knew I liked the idea of helping others. I enjoyed learning about electricity. I even tried a basic electronics course at Ward School of Electronics, but couldn't keep up with the math. I liked carpentry, but I didn't love it and after my experience working as a lineman in the winter months, I figured I wasn't going to find working as a carpenter in the coming winter season any better.

It didn't dawn on me to consider forming my own construction company, or obtaining my real estate license and partaking in what would become one of the greatest periods of growth on Cape Cod. It took me a while to learn to think outside the box.

I was stuck with the idea of wearing a white shirt and tie and making a lot of money. You might observe some issues with my thinking. Like maybe, you could become a millionaire without wearing a white shirt and tie? In my book *Relationships Open Doors,* I discuss that along with my sales careers, I also did end up teaching quite often for business subjects. So my original major, education, wasn't a total waste.

I finally met with Wayne Wall at his Hartford office. As you might imagine, he painted a glorious picture of working at the Travelers, especially for the Group Insurance Division. It sounded great. Although, I still felt maybe I was jumping on Jim Maloney's "train."

I really wanted to find a different company. Growing up near Hartford, Travelers Tower could be seen from twenty to thirty miles away.

It represented that Hartford in the era was considered the insurance capital of the world and it was booming.

Still, there were other companies in the city. I kept searching and then Wayne called my house. My mother called me on the Cape and suggested I come home and take the position and the school.

Chapter XX

October 26, 1970, Quarry vs. Ali;
heading to the Boston Garden with Joe Pierce.

On October 26, 1970, Joe Pierce and I drove to Boston and went to Boston Garden to watch the Muhammed Ali vs. "Fighting Irish" Jerry Quarry heavyweight boxing match with thousands of Irish American guys from "Southie": South Boston.

I hoped I didn't run into my Velvet Hammer buddy with the distorted nose.

Early in the summer, I was wondering how I would get to Atlanta to see the fight. The large screens set up in the Garden weren't the same, but saved a long drive. Muhammed won the bout on a technicality. The fight was stopped in the third round.

There were thunderous boos and curses from the Boston crowd. Calls of Quarry throwing the fight, being a bum, and more, echoed throughout the Garden. Actually, *The Ring* magazine had Quarry as the Number one-rated heavyweight contender, and he was the WBA's Number three-rated contender.

He was by no means a bum. The match and

outcome just proved that Ali was, truly, "The Greatest"!

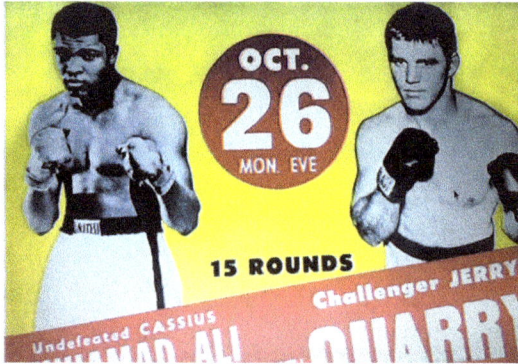

Hey I told him I was going to be there.
I'm sure he remembered, Right?

Many years later I learned that Muhammed Ali was part Irish himself. I'm not sure why it didn't come out during the lead up to the Quarry fight. It probably wasn't politically correct in the era, but Muhammed's maternal great grandfather Abe Grady was born in Ennis, County Clare, Ireland. In the 1860s, he decided to immigrate to America, and settled in Kentucky, where he met and married an African American woman. who had been freed from slavery. They had a daughter who grew up and married Cassius Clay, Sr. In 1942, Cassius Jr. was born. I believe Ali did end up going back to Ennis a couple of times.

Chapter XXI

I Found a Job!!

The next morning I called Wayne Wall and made an appointment to go for an interview in Hartford. John, Spike's brother-in-law was bummed, as there was still plenty of work to be done on the building. Spike had to return to California and John was now working full time on the building. The college kids went back to school, so there was a shortage of cheap labor.

I had to wear a white shirt and tie. I accepted a position with the Travelers for their Group Insurance Division, with "sort of" a guarantee I would be assigned to New Haven, CT, branch after a paid year in their Insurance School.

This would also prove to be significant as I hadn't majored in Business, and I found a company willing to pay me to learn their business. The only glitch was the fact that the next school didn't start till February. I decided to give my notice to John that I would be leaving at the end of October. So that was it.

I withdrew my savings from the bank, said goodbye, and headed home. School started in February, which gave me a chance to catch up on much-needed rest. I never really stopped and rested for over three years in order to finish college as fast as I could, while substitute teaching often.

Fran Macchi, one of the Macchi Shoe Store owner's sons and St. Mary alums in Connecticut, told me that in the '60s, if you were twenty-one, had a military ID and were attending an accredited college, you were allowed to substitute teach. This was unique to Connecticut.

Fran substituted at East Hartford High during my senior year. I also worked some evenings., weekends, and summers as a dispatcher for the Hartford Automobile Club. I would take a midnight to seven shift on Friday and Saturday nights, bringing a sleeping bag so I could catch some sleep after doing my homework.

Thanks to my elementary school friend Tommy Connolly, whom I mentioned meeting early on at Central and getting into the Veterans Club, along with Ronnie Perham, Brian Hope, and Bruce Chamberlain. Tommy Connolly also gave me his Canada Dry route in the greater New Britain during weekends. It was like having a franchise. Oh, and I painted a few houses. I'm almost out of breath writing about it all. My sojourn on the Cape was fun, but I still worked, and worked hard. I needed a rest before I started the rest of my life.

I entered the Travelers Insurance School in February and found an interesting apartment in Manchester. The apartment complex was modeled after a California design mainly for singles, with a pool, recreation rooms, pool tables, lounge, and paddle tennis. I had a great rapport with the manager, and he agreed to allow me to live rent-free in exchange for bringing new tenants. I found at least one new tenant every month, thus I lived rent-free.

The Travelers Group school was both informative and fun. In March, during the second month of the school I stepped out for a coffee and heard "Jimmy Naughton!"

There in front of me was our high school class of '62 Class President Frank Sola. I mean, *what are the odds?* Frank had gone to college right after graduation, got his degree and obtained a very coveted sales job with IBM, the best tech company of the era. I thought I was doing so great attending school for the Travelers, but here was Frank already out of college four or five years, and working for possibly the best technology company in the US.

I continued thinking *maybe I screwed up.* Maybe I should have tried to get into school right away. Frank did it the traditional way, he graduated from high school and went to college and landed a good career in his early 20s. However, I was convinced that I could never get into college because of my low SAT Scores.

We're all different. I'm just presenting thoughts and situations using my personal experience to convince a young man or woman that regardless of your individual situation, your life circumstances, you can achieve your dreams and goals. Your dreams and goals are yours and you may have to proceed differently to obtain them. You could be deciding to go back to school in your 40s or 50s. Who cares? It's *your* life. You can decide to be successful at any age. That's between you and God, our Father. I tell you what I did in this book and in my other books, the good and the not-so-good.

There are many who have been a great deal more successful than me; in fact, Frank Sola left IBM and started his own successful tech company. We met by chance at Christy's in Newport, twenty years later, in the late nineties, as he was celebrating the sale of his company!

In previous books I have pointed out that sometimes the well-intentioned positive thinking books on the market get us all excited to do something. But then what? In this book and in my first two, I try to provide a step-by-step description of what I did and how I did it under often very difficult circumstances. I also provide information on the different jobs I worked at so that my younger readers get an inside look at careers they might otherwise never learn about.

You probably know that not everyone is willing to share personal information with the world in order to help the world. I am, and I will. When you read my story, I believe you will be motivated to begin!

Not everyone gets the luxury to grow up in a normal supportive home with plenty of money to pay for one's education. By the way, there is nothing wrong with that! It's what I tried to do for my kids. I didn't have that, so I hope to help those kids whose situations are more like mine. Having said that, there are many parts to this book that will be of help to anyone who is trying to get ahead in life and business. Often you must have to experiment—try different things—to figure out what you want to do in life. Does what you want require extra training or dedication? If it does, you must find a way to pay for these.

For some of you, it could take a while, as it did for me. So I finished school at age 26, four or five years later than many of my classmates. But I did it: I graduated! Maybe I could have gone another route to accomplish my goals and that would have been fine as well.

I did have a difficult time adjusting to corporate life. After reading my stories, you can understand. I have described growing up in a blue-collar home, in a very blue-collar manufacturing town, with lots of blue-collar friends. My college experience was not conducive to learning how to "fit in" corporately, meaning I lived at home and hung around one of the many factory bars near Pratt & Whitney or the Willow Inn. It's not what most would consider a great college experience. Thus, the corporate world proved to be a real challenge for me.

I owed a lot to the Travelers instructors for

their help and patience and I eventually graduated
from their school. It's a shame that companies
don't offer intensive training and schools like
in the old days. I found it a great way to begin a
career after college

Chapter XXII

Getting married: Life beginning to move quickly.

During training, I met a young, pretty executive assistant to a rising vice president. Actually, I was introduced to Sharon by my childhood friend Jim Maloney, who was already into his second year at the Travelers. We hit it off from the very start and I asked her to marry me. Knowing that it was possible that I could be assigned anywhere in the country, we decided to set our wedding date in August. It was strongly rumored that I was going to be assigned to the New Haven Office, which would mean that my future bride Sharon would be able to keep her great job with one of the senior vice presidents in the Group Department.

The idea of staying close to home appealed to me and to Sharon, as we both had elderly parents. Her mother was a recent widow, and all of our relatives and friends lived in the area.

With little time, we and her mom planned a huge wedding at the Willimantic Country Club. Both of us had tons of friends and relatives and I think we invited them all.

One of the neighbors in my apartment complex

145

said if he got an invitation he would supply
the band. Dave Califano (name changed), my
apartment neighbor, was from Springfield, and we
called him Mafia Dave due to the way he carried
himself, his friends, his mysterious weekly drives
in his black Cadillac to Providence, etc.

We didn't have a band yet. Why not? Dave was
invited. I remember asking the band leader if he
could play "Unchained Melody" by the Righteous
Brothers for our wedding dance? He replied, "we
will play anything you like, as the instruments are
owned by that guy," as he motioned towards Mafia
Dave.

So they played a terrific rendition of our song.
I know what you're thinking, "First he is employed
by a member of the Witness Protection Program,
and now here's his free wedding band. This guy
can't get away from the mob—and he's Irish!"

Dave came in with a white suit, black shirt,
white tie, and a Panama hat which accented
his black hair and Sicilian complexion. He also
brought not one but two dates. If that wasn't
enough, within twenty minutes he was at our
wedding table inquiring about the pretty blonde
who just came in. The girl was my New York
cousin JP's wife, Pat, whom Sharon thought looked
like Grace Kelly. I'm thinking, *You gotta be kidding
me!*

He proceeded to ask about the appropri-
ateness of asking her out on the dance floor. With
zero hesitation, I said, "Dave, that's my cousin's

wife. He's a hard hat, a steamfitter and a former leader of an Irish Gang in Washington Heights and the 6'4" guy standing next to him? That's his brother. You even look sideways at that gal and this hall will go up in flames. You understand Dave, don't ya?"

He did. Shortly after the wedding I was told Dave and a bunch of his friends were in jail for supposedly holding up a tractor-trailer full of fur coats on the Mass Pike. I do not know if that was true. *Whew!!* Was a free band worth it? Yeah, it was—then!

I should mention that Sharon's wedding party had presented me with an unusual pre-wedding gift. I mentioned previously that I owned an Austin Healey 3000 shortly before we met, however, out of financial necessity a few months earlier, I had downsized and was driving my deceased uncles '62 Chevy Impala, which I had to start with a screwdriver across the solenoid. So for a goof they gave me a pre-wedding gift, neatly wrapped in a small box, which contained a gold painted screwdriver!

I was too numb and nervous to be embarrassed. I was overwhelmed at the time. All of a sudden life started moving quickly. I graduated from college, although later than most, a new career, and getting married soon! *Jump in and start swimming!* (The name of my first book.) I couldn't even begin to imagine how overwhelmed Sharon and her poor widowed mother was.

I know my readers are getting tired of me saying how I don't believe in coincidences, but then end up telling you of the many in my life. Well, we had the traditional bride tossing her bouquet to some hopeful female guests. My cousin Patsy Kelly from Ireland who was spending the summer with my mother caught it. The question is, who caught the garter?

Remember early on in the story when I heard someone call out, "Hey Jimmy!" my first day on Central's campus? Yep! My St. Mary's Kindergarten and Central Connecticut Veteran Fraternity friend, Tommy Connolly. He put the garter on my cousin Patsy.

August 21, 1971. The garter. My cousin Patsy from Ireland with my St. Mary's and Central CT Veterans Club brother, Tommy Connolly! This was one fun wedding!!

The owner of the Willow Inn, where I hung out

during college, when I wasn't working or studying, Frank Benetieri, organized a $1.00 Dance. You needed to pin at least a dollar to dance with the bride—my bride. Corny? I think Sharon collected almost $2000 from that dance: a huge sum, back in the day. Years later, I probably would have thought, *is this tacky?* Maybe, but we were starting off poor back then.

We changed clothes, kissed everyone goodbye and headed to Cape Cod for our "Motor Honeymoon," counting our gifts along the way.

The following morning we took a ride to Provincetown. We no sooner parked our car when another car pulled up next to ours. Unbelievably, it was Jenny Napolitano and her husband Frank Contois from East Hartford. I was introduced to Jenny by Judy Thibodeau, who I went to St. Mary's with. Both great gals! I knew Frank through my friend John Choquette as they both worked at a shoe store in the Manchester Mall during our final year at Central. Are you thinking *How does this stuff happen to him?*

I, in turn, introduced Sharon, and told them of our wedding the day before. They invited us to go for lunch on the water. They also insisted on picking up the bill. What were the odds?

I heard years later that Jenny and Frank moved to Colchester, CT. Years later, Jenny got involved in politics and eventually got elected Mayor.

The next evening we attended a dinner concert with the Four Tops at the Melody Tent in Hyannis.

As dinner began, an announcement came over the speakers that there was a '62 Chevy with Connecticut license plates in the parking lot with its lights on. There were only about a thousand guests waiting to see who was the owner of the car. Nope, I wasn't nervous! I shrewdly waited a few minutes and excused myself to go to the men's room. RIP, Jenny.

So that's what took place after college.

When reminiscing about all this, the question that dawned on me was *If I went to work for the other large giant insurance company in Hartford, The Aetna. Would Sharon and I have met?* At the time, she lived with her recently widowed mother in Willimantic. I never went to Willimantic, and she didn't go to clubs.

I know this. For my last semester, I needed fifteen credits or five courses. Even with that credit load, I knew I needed some electives, i.e., swimming, or art courses that I could take in the June four-week summer semester to satisfy the rest of my Bachelor's degree requirement. It was imperative that I pass every course. I always liked geography when I was a kid, so I thought I would take a geography course as one of my electives for the last semester.

It turned out that the course I selected was meant for graduate students working on their masters. I soon realized that the only non-graduate student in the class was me! *Oh, Great!* The professor had a doctorate degree and came from the CIA to teach. There was to be only a "mid-term" and a "final exam," plus two projects. He gave us a sample quiz in the beginning to provide us with the type of questions we would see on the two exams. I flunked it badly as did most of the class. Oh, oh: As I said, I needed to pass this course and all of my courses to graduate, or at least complete my BA degree requirement, in June.

If I flunked one, it most likely would cause me to have to attend the fall semester and that would prevent me from applying for a career until January of the following year plus it would depend on the timing of the next Group Insurance School. It was a big concern as I was older than most of the kids. I needed to graduate and get a job. If that happened, meaning if my graduation got extended, I now wonder, would Sharon and I have met?

In looking back it seemed like Fate was pushing us to get together. So here's what happened. I began working on the first project. I remember being at the Raymond Library in my hometown of East Hartford, when suddenly I felt someone tap me on the shoulder as I was looking through index cards. Turning around to see this short (at 5'7", I'm short, so you get it) dark haired kid staring at me. "Yeah? What's up?" I whispered. (No talking allowed.)

The kid then says, "it looks like you are taking Human Geography by the CIA Professor at Central." *That's right,* says I. "You're never going to pass it!" Mind you, I had never seen this kid in my life. *What?* He then said, "I took the course and was one of the few students to pass it. I can help you. You want my help?" I was speechless.

Although this type of thing has happened to me before. *Who is this guy?* I thought. He then told me he was parked out front and that if I wanted, I should follow him to his house. He lived on the outskirts of town near the Manchester town line.

I remember going into his parents ranch home passing through acres of undeveloped land.

I was so intent on keeping up with him, I didn't pay any attention to names of streets along the way, thus I had no idea where I was. It felt weird. I mean I didn't know this guy. First he gave me the two projects that he completed a year ago. Obviously I couldn't use them, but they helped put things in perspective and gave me a clearer understanding of what the professor was looking for. Then he gave me a set of study notes that he had put together for both exams. He said, "study these and you should do OK."

I was extremely skeptical. *What is going on here?* I thought. I got a B on my first and second projects. I got a B on the mid-term, and I received a B on the final. Fifty percent of the class failed. I know the term geography doesn't sound as difficult as calculus, but this professor and this course were brutal. I finished my BA in June! My question to myself later on in life was similar to the Aetna question.

If I didn't meet this kid, would I have met and married my wife? Would I have had children, grandchildren? As I said, every course that last semester was crucial in me being able to begin looking for a career. As I also mentioned earlier, it was difficult to find jobs in 1970. If I did eventually get into the Travelers would she have already married the guy she was dating? If he had his way, they might have.

Maybe I had this feeling and these questions due to all my reading while working on the Cape? Titles like *The Strangest Secret,* by Earl Nightingale, *There is a River,* by Edgar Cayce, *Think and Grow Rich*, by Napoleon Hill, *Psycho Cybernetics*, by Dr. Maxwell Maltz, and more.

They say timing is everything! It's crazy, but did Human Geography hold one of the keys to my future? Was the Central student who I had never seen before, not in school and not in town, sent to me, to us, to move things in my life, along?

I guess if it was just this one instance, I wouldn't question, but there have been many similar happenings during my life.

My best educated guess? *Yes!*

Chapter XXIII

My new career at the Travelers begins.

Bummer! I didn't get the New Haven assignment. Instead, I was told to report to the Princeton/Trenton Travelers Office. We were both a little numb. Sharon would have to give up her super executive assistant job and tell her widowed mother we were going to be living about four and a half hours away. My parents were devastated also. We didn't have a lot of time to dwell on things. We had to report within a week.

I met my new boss, Larry O'Brien, for breakfast at Howard Johnson on Rt. 1, just outside Princeton and Trenton. About fifteen minutes into our meeting I happened to glance down at my shoes. *OMG!* One was black and the other brown.

Going to the Men's room was not an option.

In my earlier books I share a story of me showing up for my first branch meeting in a brokerage office with Nike sneakers, as I had forgotten to pack my shoes for the trip.

I still get a twinge in my stomach when I think of these embarrassing moments, even now, knowing how insignificant they were. That's life!

Humans worry about the small stuff, even though we know we needn't.

I noted that we shared our office building with a company called Addressograph Multigraph. At my first opportunity to bump into their local manager, I asked about a high-school friend who grew up one street over: Johnny Sullivan, East Hartford High, Class of '61. Johnny didn't go to college. He instead got a job as a repairman for Addressograph Multigraph, covering some Hartford accounts.

This company was a precursor to computers; it provided machinery that produced client account info on metal plates, kind of like a giant typewriter. One night he was with our group at the previously mentioned KayRock Inn. He would always have to leave a contact number in case one of his accounts had an emergency.

That night he got a call, but it was for someone else's account—Pratt & Whitney Aircraft was experiencing problems with one of their machines. Apparently, their rep was unable to be located. Johnny left immediately.

He had a great personality and P&W was so impressed they requested that he be their account representative. From that position, he soon threw his hat in the mix for a sales job.

It was now five years later and this manager is telling me that Johnny was just promoted to President of Addressograph Multigraph.

Unbelievable! I remember telling Sharon, here
I was so proud about going back to school later
in life, graduating and getting into the Traveler's
Insurance School and Johnny'd just been
promoted to President of a national company! Not
even thirty years old, and never been to college.

Again, it's OK to acknowledge that, but as
I said, we were all different. We just need to
do our own thing. "Do" is the important word!
Could anything like this happen today—move up
in a company without a degree as Johnny did?
Anything is possible. Best to have insurance, and
get a degree, or more education.

I never forgot it, and thought it a great example
of Earl Nightingale's theory that "we become what
we think about." He always talked about becoming
wealthy, seeing himself driving a nice car, buying a
beautiful home. Like many of us, his family had to
work hard to put bread on the table. They lived in
an apartment next door to the Credit Union. I last
saw Johnny in Newport at Christie's in the early
'90s. He was celebrating the purchase of one of
Newport's mansions!

He said he was sending his corporate jet
around the country to bring some of his old class
of '61 buddies to his high school reunion.

I lost track of him after that, and I know it
was about the time computers were hitting the
corporate landscape like wildfire. Nothing lasts
forever!

Coincidence alert: A little ways down, you will learn about another East Hartford classmate, Frank Sola, celebrating his success at Christie's a few years later.

Around that time frame, also while partying at Christie's Newport with John Choquette and his wife, Marti Driscoll Choquette, we bumped into Ginger Crowe, I think from Class of '63. She had her own business and looked elegant.

Note: When I talk about partying at Christie's, I am really saying we were there weekends throughout the decade of the nineties, to listen and dance to our friend, Rhode Island's own "Jimmy Buffett," Alger Mitchell, who performed there every weekend. We are fortunate to live about twenty minutes away.

Whether it was Island music, Irish music, Country, or Rock n' Roll, Alger sang it all—and better, as far as my friends and I were concerned! In the mid nineties, I introduced him to our class president Frank Sola, who I earlier mentioned last meeting outside the Travelers in 1971.

He was now celebrating the sale of his company with some Wall Street friends of mine on the deck at Christie's in Newport, Rhode Island.

The nineties were a fun decade for us, and my kids complained we had more fun than they did. Of course, we occasionally brought them on Christie's deck as Alger played over the water with spectacular scenery, yachts and sunsets in the back of his stage.

Alger also performed at our Christmas and Summer pool parties in that era and before. It was a blast, and we all miss that fun time.

Back to my first after-college job at The Travelers Insurance Company. I was initially assigned some existing smaller group insurance accounts to service, in addition to an assigned area to work on for new business.

Back then, every company needed group health and life insurance to offer to their employees, so I had to convince insurance brokers to give me the opportunity to quote on their customer's plans using price, coverage and promised better service.

I was responsible for central New Jersey. Sharon landed another great job at the Wall Street Journal, so we were on our way. I went to Real Estate license training evenings so I could sell units in our complex, and I also sold men's and boys' clothes at a Jewish Men's and Boys' clothing store, part time, evenings and Saturdays.

I discuss this in more detail in my book *Relationships Open Doors,* from *Amazon.com.*

Note: This clothing salesman position was the only job I ever got fired from, and I was the store's Number One salesman, plus I was only part-time. {You need to read the book.) You also are realizing that I wasn't afraid to work hard to obtain my goal.

Sharon and I joined the Princeton YMCA and played Racquetball two or three times a week.

She was a quick learner and we both got great workouts.

I was not enamoured with my first job out of college.

Chapter XXIV

Moving on up! My careers.

I have written extensively on my careers in my books *Jump In and Start Swimming,* and a sequel, *Relationships Open Doors.* The following is a brief overview of my careers that I have written about in those books. Maybe some of these, along with my earlier banking, lineman, construction jobs, might be of interest to my younger readers.

You may contact me through my book website *www.KeyPublishingCompany.com,* and I will try to help with your job and career decisions.

I left The Travelers on great terms to move back to Connecticut and start selling insurance directly as an independent agent representing many companies, including The Travelers. Initially I was selling automobile and homeowner's insurance, along with life insurance and small group insurance contracts..

As you may recall, my first job after graduating Central Connecticut State University was with The Travelers. I spent a year in their group insurance school, so now I was becoming an expert in all lines of insurance.

While out canvassing I bumped into Al Ambrose, Class of '63—a great guy and a terrific athlete, whom I last saw playing basketball at Martin Park the summer of 1962. (You might recall an earlier scene of me waving to some guys playing basketball at Martin Park while trying to maneuver my '52 Dodge Ram and crashing simultaneously into two cars. He was one of them.)

He had graduated from college, gotten married, and started in the insurance business. It was almost ten years later. After attending a training program with Liberty Mutual, he was out selling commercial insurance. I listened to him over a cup of coffee, and it was like I'd last seen him the day before, instead of ten years ago. As I have said, I still feel that way when I meet up with my former East Hartford friends.

I decided that if I was going to grow my business, I better start trying to obtain commercial accounts, so every day, either in the morning or afternoon, I went and knocked on business doors for about two hours. It paid off. First I landed a gas station, and then an optical business in the center of East Hartford.

Noticing my aggressiveness, my Aetna Representative offered to refer me to attend the Aetna Property Casualty School for a couple of months. (More relationship building and networking—Read the book!) It was considered the best property casualty insurance school in the country, thus it was an honor to get accepted, and I did.

Unknown to me, a few of the large mutual insurance companies had recently made the decision to move into the property casualty arena and to begin marketing automobile and homeowners policies in addition to their traditional life insurance products.

I worked hard as an agent, learned a lot, and was in a hurry to make a lot of money. The insurance business takes time and patience in addition to the hard work of getting clients. Metropolitan Life Insurance Company heard of my background and contacted me about joining them as a consultant and instructor for their new mini home office in Warwick, RI.

At the time I had gained a ton of experience with all the different insurance products, along with how to market and sell them.

I wore many hats at The Met. First I traveled the New England states with other instructors, teaching and preparing their representatives to take and pass their states' casualty and property insurance exam. It was different for each state.

Then I would present to agent invitees from around New England in the company's recently established Career Success School in Warwick, RI.

There I would teach product knowledge plus how-tos for selling homeowners and automobile insurance policies along with their traditional life insurance products.

Often, in the evenings, I would make sales calls with their agents in the field. One of the projects I helped them with (there was actually a small team of us who were part of the Met Career Success School) was the setting up of a telemarketing operation.

In those days, the large telephone companies had a financial interest and access to a number of experts in areas like telemarketing, plus big expense accounts. So I ended up with an abundance of more expertise in this area, which in turn made me more valuable.

At around that time, Rhode Island's major newspaper, the *Providence Journal*, was beginning to sell their newspaper via phone. As I mentioned early on, I was a paper delivery boy in my youth. In those days one of my responsibilities was acquiring new customers, in addition to delivery.

Now the industry was selling/obtaining customers by phone. A neighbor who knew of my recently obtained telemarketing knowledge submitted my name to his friend at the paper. After my first interview, I was hired to co- manage the *Journal*'s new telemarketing department. It was a part-time position, three evenings and a half day Saturday.

I told my wife the hardest part of the job was Friday evenings, when I would have to terminate some of our telemarketers who could not make their weekly quotas. Some had families and needed the extra income. I hated that I couldn't help them. I realized quickly that while I always believed that selling can be taught, selling via phone, especially cold calling, is something you need to have in you. You either have it or you don't.

Visiting Jimmy Maloney at his new home Dallas, Summer 1981. Both married, with babies, new careers, new futures. Reminiscing about the past, and the previous crazy last twenty years. Two blue collar Baby Boomers from East Hartford "moving on up"! My daughter Erin had locked onto the song and sang it continuously all over Dallas. "Ooh Driving my life away, looking for a better way..." Eddie Rabbitt, June, 1980

During my employment, I was proud that the Providence Journal was ranked Number One out of ten thousand newspapers in the US for obtaining new customers! (Later on, both of my sons worked for the telemarketing department and successfully sold newspapers for the *Journal* while in college.)

For my young job seekers, note how I moved on up with the help of friends , neighbors and anyone else. I describe this as "relationship building" in great detail in my book and sequel *Relationships Open Doors,* available at Amazon. My book website is *www.KeyPublishingCompany.com.*

Chapter XXV

Wall Street. My career begins to skyrocket!

A friend, a.k.a. a relationship, in Boston, set me up with a job interview during the Fall of 1980 with a Wall Street firm, Dean Witter Reynolds (now Morgan Stanley).

Actually, as I thought about it, it was Jim Maloney who said he had a friend who was formerly in the insurance business and was now working in Boston for a Wall Street firm. That started me thinking. "What does Wall Street want with an insurance guy?" As it turned out, because the decade of the '70s had little movement in the stock market, very few stocks were sold; thus they were looking into getting to other areas to bring in assets and allow their brokers (advisors) to earn some commisions. As it turned out they decided to market annuities, traditionally an insurance "payout product."

Everyone from that era remembers the tv ad "When EF Hutton speaks, people listen!" EF Hutton was the first brokerage firm to market this new investment type of annuity. Soon, Dean Witter and other brokerage firms decided to emphasize the accumulation part of the product which allowed for tax deferred growth of principal.

With interest rates in the double digits in that era, the single premium annuity, along with its tax deferral feature, quickly became very much in demand—but it had to be sold, and as the cliché says, "If it sounds too good to be true, it probably is." I turned the opportunity down initially, but luckily, they persisted, and I began a new career as an internal annuity wholesaler.

As mentioned, I write more extensively on this career in my earlier books. I also wrote in my book, *Jump In and Start Swimming*, that I told the recruiter we had young babies, never traveled, knew nothing about Wall Street, and therefore, I would have to decline Dean Witter's offer.

Regional Vice President James Dwyer, who was silently listening on the call unbeknown to me, chimed in and said in a raspy voice "Naughton you're not going to make that decision right now! You're going to go to Green Airport in the morning and pick up tickets for a flight to La Guardia. There will be a car waiting to take you to 5 World Trade Center. You will have a half hour interview and then you can decide!" I found myself nodding in agreement at the phone, like *please don't hurt me I'll do what you want!* (Just kidding.)

I told my wife "I think I might be working for the mob." I flew to NYC the next morning and accepted the offer after about fifteen minutes, and it changed our lives in many positive ways forever.

As I walked out of the conference room,

I glanced at the large picture windows, and I noticed the Hudson River, then the Statue of Liberty, and Ellis Island where my folks landed so long ago, and my eyes filled up.

Don't try this! Don't tell a firm you don't want the job until you're really certain it's not for you. You are reading about true Destiny, Fate, The Hand of God. It was me, but it wasn't me. All I wanted in that era was to find a way to make $25,000. Instead, I made $80,000 my first year. Just the beginning!

On December 1, 1980, with zero Wall Street or brokerage experience, I was assigned to the New England/Upstate New York Territory, which unfortunately—or fortunately!—was last, #14 out 14/ A few months later they added Pittsburgh, State College and Scranton.

I apologize if it sounds like bragging, but I took the territory to the Number One position by the end of the first year, and it remained there during my tenure.

Maybe not at the time, but can you see the advantage of taking over the worst or last territory? I mean where could I have gone if I took Number One? Maybe down!

I was promoted to Regional Vice President, and became the DWR "Man of The Year." I was flown with Sharon to the edge of space above Scotland on the Concorde and received many awards, including a plaque from Rhode Island's Sen. Claiborne Pell. You need to read my book

Relationships Open Doors, a sequel to *Jump In and Start Swimming*. Relationships and networking are absolutely necessary attributes you, as a student, are going to have to acquire. It's *imperative* in order to get a job, a career, *and* to advance.

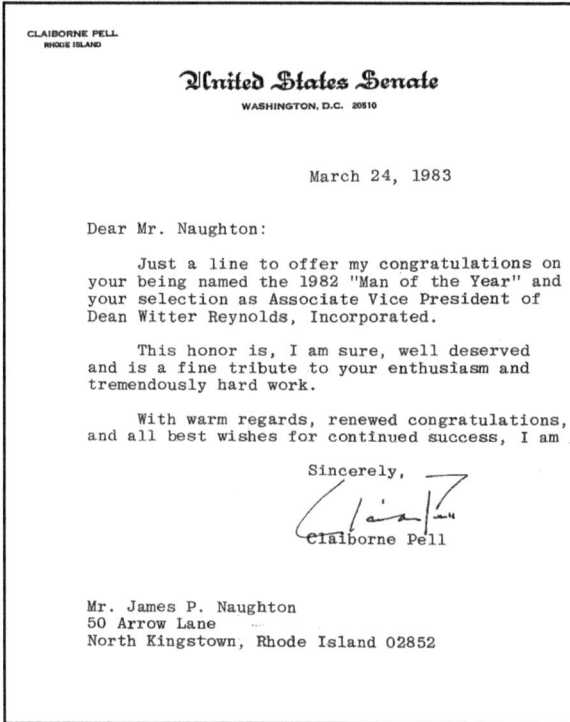

CLAIBORNE PELL
RHODE ISLAND

United States Senate
WASHINGTON, D.C. 20510

March 24, 1983

Dear Mr. Naughton:

Just a line to offer my congratulations on your being named the 1982 "Man of the Year" and your selection as Associate Vice President of Dean Witter Reynolds, Incorporated.

This honor is, I am sure, well deserved and is a fine tribute to your enthusiasm and tremendously hard work.

With warm regards, renewed congratulations, and all best wishes for continued success, I am

Sincerely,

Claiborne Pell

Mr. James P. Naughton
50 Arrow Lane
North Kingstown, Rhode Island 02852

Note the news article's mention of Elin Pye, bottom left. Elin, while she didn't get a lot of mention, was an employee of the oldest mutual fund company in the US, Massachusetts Financial Services Co., MFS, and in keeping with my philosophy of relationship building and networking. I did include Elin, and later on I became a Regional Vice President at MFS.

Treat everyone, even competitors with respect! You never know! Later on, you will see a letter to me from an industry leader about how I handled the competition.

By the way, is that *really* my hair?

May 8, 1981
The Tribune, Scranton, Pa.

ANNUITY SEMINAR — Dean Witter Reynolds, Inc., 211 North Washington Ave., investment security firm, held an annuity seminar Thursday at the Downtown Holiday Inn. James Naughton, Dean Witter Reynolds vice president, spoke on annuities. From left: John M. Egan, vice president, Mid Atlantic Region; Naughton; Jean Briskey, operations manager and assistant treasurer; William Comerford, vice president, investments.
(Tribune photo — Olds)

300 Get Reynolds Tips For Quadrupling Money

By PETE GRADY

There's always an audience when money talks. Money talked Thursday night at the Downtown Holiday Inn, where over 300 persons listened to a Dean Witter Reynolds insurance specialist explain the value of tax-deferred annuities.

James Naughton, vice president of Dean Witter Reynolds, the second largest investment firm on Wall Street, with a branch office in Scranton since 1938,

Elin Pye, a financial expert with Massachusetts Financial Services, an investment firm dealing in managing money.

Keep in mind that when I first had to get up and present at my college Public Speaking Class, I froze like an ice sculpture. The professor asked if I knew the Lord's Prayer. I said "of course." He then asked me to say it, which I did with no problem. He made the point that "When you know something, and really know it, like the Lord's Prayer. It's easy to speak it in front of a group."

In the beginning of my DWR career, I created a public seminar for my broker's (now called Financial Advisors) clients and prospects and one which I could teach stockbrokers to do on their own, as I was only in their branch office once a month, if that much. As you can tell in the newspaper article above, I wasn't a frozen ice sculpture any longer.

That night, I was in front of three hundred attendees, including three news reporters copying every word! (Most of my hour-long talk was intentionally removed from the article for this book. It can be made available when and if appropriate. I'm sure today it would not meet the approval of FINRA (used to be NASD). A few years later, I spoke in front of one thousand financial consultants at a Merrill-Lynch Convention at the Innsbruck Golf Resort in Tampa, Florida (I could teach you with "my tricks of the trade" to do the same in about one hour).

It's rare in the business world to get a letter like the one on the next page, especially when you're "moving on up" to another firm. I will keep reminding my high-school and college readers of the earlier picture of my project, the United Homes, and, a little further down, the one of my SATs along with my stomach problems, and of course, the crazy stories of my unique "college campus," The Willow Inn.

There is absolutely no reason that any of you could not achieve the same and more!

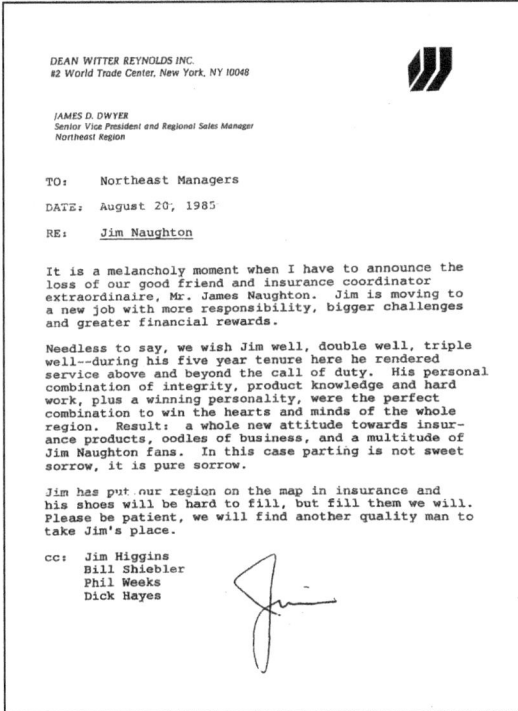

DEAN WITTER REYNOLDS INC.
#2 World Trade Center, New York, NY 10048

JAMES D. DWYER
Senior Vice President and Regional Sales Manager
Northeast Region

TO: Northeast Managers

DATE: August 20, 1985

RE: Jim Naughton

It is a melancholy moment when I have to announce the loss of our good friend and insurance coordinator extraordinaire, Mr. James Naughton. Jim is moving to a new job with more responsibility, bigger challenges and greater financial rewards.

Needless to say, we wish Jim well, double well, triple well--during his five year tenure here he rendered service above and beyond the call of duty. His personal combination of integrity, product knowledge and hard work, plus a winning personality, were the perfect combination to win the hearts and minds of the whole region. Result: a whole new attitude towards insurance products, oodles of business, and a multitude of Jim Naughton fans. In this case parting is not sweet sorrow, it is pure sorrow.

Jim has put our region on the map in insurance and his shoes will be hard to fill, but fill them we will. Please be patient, we will find another quality man to take Jim's place.

cc: Jim Higgins
      Bill Shiebler
      Phil Weeks
      Dick Hayes

President Calvin Coolidge said it better: "Press on. Nothing in the world can take the place of persistence. Talent will not; nothing is more common than unsuccessful men with talent. Education alone will not; the world is full of educated derelicts. Persistence and determination alone are all powerful."

So, from a tip from my childhood friend Jim Maloney regarding Wall Street looking for insurance guys, my career and life turned around in a fantastic manner. Remember when I discussed earlier in the book meeting and marrying my wife Sharon at The Travelers? He introduced us! Remember also, early on when John Choquette and I were deciding on going back to school full time? It was Jim who enrolled into the University of Hartford after his active duty in the Navy ended—the first from our crew to do so. He gave us the courage to do the same.

Think about your friends and their parents when you are making similar decisions. It's part of the networking and relationship building which I suggested you learn more about.

As I wrote in *Jump In and Start Swimming*, I was on a roll, and it didn't go unnoticed in the industry. Moving on up! I was offered, and accepted, a position of Regional Vice President for America's oldest mutual fund company Massachusetts Financial Services, MFS, Jan 1, 1987, responsible for the sales of Mutual Funds, Annuities, 401k and later, separately managed accounts for New England.

As I have written in my books, if I wasn't Number One in sales in any given year, I was in the top three. In 2000, I became Number One in the industry of 18,000 wholesalers bringing in close to a billion dollars in a single year!

My accomplishments are described more completely in *Jump In and Start Swimming*. Again, I show these awards in order to back up my premise that *you can become successful* regardless of your past or current challenging circumstances.

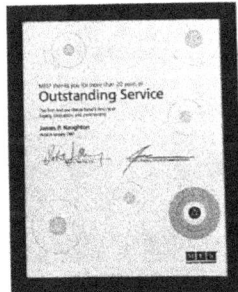

Some of Jim's Number One Producer- MVP awards and his induction into the Hall Of Fame

These along with three Rolex watches, pewter cups, plaques and trips are just a few!

20 years of cups for being among the highest producers of his firm

Lapis Globe, a Heritage award
for being a team player

Number One producer, 1995
The bowl awarded to the number one producer
was replaced with Rolex watches in later years.
In addition to the Silver Bowl, Jim was awarded
3 Rolex watches during his 20-year career

Prestigious Chairman's Club member's Mug

Enlarged version of the Top producers cup-shown
above awarded in Jim's last full year in the field, 2007

I borrowed this letter from my first book *Jump In and Start Swimming*, written for my speech to

University of Rhode Island Juniors and Seniors.
I also wanted to give the students a glimpse of
how I handled the competition: Decently and
respectfully, the same way I would want to be
treated. I was rewarded big time!

In this situation I had given some advice and
help to a new young wholesaler at Alliance Capital
who was finding it difficult getting into some
Boston Brokerage Offices. I then contacted his
company and told them what a great job he was
doing.

AllianceCapital

Alliance Fund
Distributors, Inc.
1345 Avenue of the Americas
New York, NY 10105
(212) 969-2176

April 19, 2001

Richard K. Saccullo
Executive Vice President
Head of U.S. Sales

Mr. James P. Naughton
Regional Vice President
New England
Broker/Dealer Mutual Fund Sales
Massachusetts Financial Services
500 Boylston Street
Boston, MA 02116

Dear Jim:

I had an opportunity to see the note you sent to George Keith on the rankings of our local
wholesaler in the Northeast.

In a territory that is so competitive it was a nice compliment. The fact that you took the time
to send your note says a lot about you and your personal qualities. It is no surprise MFS
is our toughest competitor.

Very truly yours,

Richard K. Saccullo
Executive Vice President
Head of US Sales

cc: George Keith

Chapter XXVI

*The Author's Formula for Success, Setbacks,
Overcoming Obstacles, Including Health Issues; questions
for the author on his choice to include
some of the crazy stories and brawls.*

My book critiquers and advisors asked why I
included the crazy stuff, the brawls etc., in this and
my other stories. Some felt it wasn't necessary.
The answer, I thought, was obvious, but in any
event, here it goes: I felt that in order to get my
underlying message of "You Can Achieve and Be
Anything You Want To Be" across to those high-
school and college students starting out in life,
who may be feeling stuck and living in tough
situations, that I have been there, that I could
relate. Because from their perspective, at least
on paper, I shouldn't have made it. But I did, and
while I didn't have the greatest book smarts, I
allowed my street smarts, the so-called "crazy
stuff," including the brawls, to toughen me up
to handle some difficult business situations and
obstacles I was to encounter.

I wanted to teach them that where there is
a will, there is truly a way! How do you do that
if you never walked in their shoes? And I think I
have. Also the wild stories are a part of the era and

179

blue-collar atmosphere I grew up in, as did many of my fellow 76,000,000 Baby Boomers!

"Life is all about making mistakes and learning from them!" —Unknown

A special thought for my high school and college readers.

We have all known guys in school who aced tests without ever seeming to pick up a book. There was always at least one of them around, gifted, and usually born with very high IQs. I WAS NOT ONE OF THEM. SCHOOL WAS STRESSFUL FOR ME! I HAD A DIFFICULT TIME IN SCHOOL. I WASN'T BORN WITH A HIGH IQ!

I invite you to bookmark this section, particularly my ALL-CAPS statements, and when you finish the book, take a look at some health issues that I had, the SAT scores I provided, and the jobs I held, then come back here and consider it all, along with my crazy Willow Inn Campus stories. Then ask yourself—and me, if I'm nearby—how did I do it? How did I graduate? How did I reach the success I attained? All I can say is, I had a GOAL. Life/God gave it to me when I was born. My goal was simple and I have stated it before: I remember being poor. I know I didn't experience the poverty my parents experienced in the "Old Country" or what many in the Third World have felt. I know my housing project was a resort compared to projects that existed then and today throughout our country.

I just knew at a young age that I didn't want to be poor. So that was my GOAL: "Not gonna be poor."

Collect bottles, deliver newspapers, make coleslaw, work in a credit union after school, climb electric light poles in a snowstorm, work as a half-ass carpenter and against all odds, with awful SAT scores, get in and graduate college while working almost full time some semesters, and then get into the business world with the help of The Travelers Insurance Company, then parlay that experience to heights of success on Wall Street that I could never imagine while hanging out at The Willow. This is what happens when you set goals and work hard.

It was a GOAL of ensuring I would not be poor. I wrote it down on a piece of paper. Sure, I read "The Strangest Secret" by Earl Nightingale and Think and Grow Rich, *by Napoleon Hill, and others, but I had my GOAL way before I ever heard of those men: I was born into it—poor. Those positive motivational pioneers just confirmed what I knew deep down and helped me to believe in myself.*

I didn't want to be poor! I was willing to work hard, often holding two jobs to attain my GOAL. I also learned from my reading how to network and to create relationships.

So there is your formula for success: Get a GOAL, learn to network and create relationships while working hard. Plus, one more thing which I will expand upon a little later on: Think Big!

BTW, hundreds, thousands have done and accomplished more than I could even conceive of, so this isn't a "look and see how great the Jimmy Naughton story is." I just happened to be willing to share my journey. In addition to preserving my story for my grandkids and great grandkids under the "How to Live Forever" theme, I'm just hoping to resonate with as many challenged young people as possible and convince them that having a GOAL is where to start.

I have had a lot of setbacks. You will too.

I don't want to dwell on mine, except to say that one of my biggest failures is that I didn't think big enough! Next time around! I also know that if I was reading this story fifty-plus years ago, I would feel that "if this guy could do it, considering all the above, I know I would too!" And that's the GOAL of this book.

Of course an equal GOAL is to convince my fellow Baby Boomers to write down a piece of their own or family history, two or three or more pages and have your grandson or daughter help you upload it for "free" as an ebook on Amazon-Kindle to preserve it FOREVER!

Since I am baring my soul, I might as well mention an obstacle that I was born with and have had to deal with from around second grade which was also a very difficult year in my young life.

In any event I developed a pain in my stomach, which I began each day with. It lasted through grammar school and into high school—probably an additional reason that I worked so much. Other than my mother, I kept it private and used a crude type of mind control to mitigate it. My family doctor said I would outgrow it, no medication.

Thanks a lot.

It affected everything in my life, but I figured I had to press on and somehow get over it. I did not disclose it to the Marines, and strangely I didn't experience the pain during my three months in Boot Camp, probably because of the chaotic shock of Parris Island. It did come back with a vengeance while in Infantry Training at Camp Geiger. Fortunately my mother sent me some canned goods that allowed me to eat something decent rather than the World War II C Rations we were fed in the field.

I had it as a lineman, forty feet up on a pole, and I endured it all the way through college. It wasn't 24/7, but it bothered me often. Drinking beer probably didn't help it. Upon arriving home from a mid-90s stressful business trip in Tucson, Arizona at 1:00 am, I threw up quite a bit of blood. Feeling wide awake I turned on the tv to one of the late night shows. Two of the guests were doctors/ scientists from Australia. They were talking about ulcers which quickly got my attention. They mentioned how they attended medical school here in the States.

They went on about how they were feeling ostracized by the US medical community, including some of their former professors. According to them, the reason for this treatment was due to their having discovered a revolutionary cause of ulcers and a cure.

Of course, I was all eyes and ears. I had

suffered for 40-plus years. They said that they proved ulcers were caused by "bugs" they called H Pylori. The good news was that, with a regimen of Pepto Bismol and antibiotics, plus a new antacid, Zantac, they said it could be cured in two weeks. *Are you kidding me?*

I called my gastroenterologist about it the next morning. He said he didn't believe it, but agreed to put me on Zantac that just became available. Fortunately, I fired him after a few weeks and found a doctor who felt comfortable administering the new treatment, as prescribed by the Australian doctors.

I took the regimen for two weeks and thankfully, unbelievably, I was cured and never have been bothered again. All those years!

It soon became accepted by all doctors across the nation. Later on, doctors confirmed that I was most likely born with an ulcer, which seemed bizarre to me. I'm sharing this not seeking pity, but again to emphasize that I can relate to those of you that have obstacles in front of your success. I didn't let it stop me from becoming successful, but it was an obstacle, you better believe it.

Again, if you're in a rough situation—poor, tough home life or you're sick, I have been there. I believe you can thrive. If you need help, you can contact me through my website *www. KeyPublishingCompany.com*

Coincidentally,, though my career was "moving on up," as soon as the ulcer left, my business started skyrocketing and never stopped!

As mentioned, this book is also a part of my "How To Live Forever Campaign Series," so it and the other four books, plus my newspaper article discussing my "Forrest Gump" trip to Woodstock, NY, in August 1969, in the series can serve as guides and examples for my fellow Baby Boomers to write down their own story, so they too can upload theirs for free as an e-book on Kindle/Amazon and preserve it and allow it to live "forever."

Also, as I previously discussed, it's equally written to inspire those kids who are in unimaginably difficult situations; who are currently in projects and can't see over the walls; who can't comprehend the possibility of a good future, or who may have health issues. It's for them that I proudly show my beginnings as the son of immigrants, initially living in the United Homes Housing Project, and my first career as an electric power lineman. These stories, combined with my other books, show a blue-collar kid living a message of "anything is possible," and how with not a lot going on for him early on, was still able to move on up. I am also humbly sharing my underwhelming SAT scores (supposedly guaranteeing that I could never get into any college).

Finally, I am including a cover photo of my first book, *Jump In and Start Swimming,* which evolved from a request to come in and provide a "spark for employment ideas" to University of Rhode Island

Juniors and Seniors who were not getting jobs due to the '08 Economic Collapse and subsequent job market crash.

The URI *Jump In Start Swimming* book also explains how I brought in close to a billion dollars in a single year. From the United Homes housing project to a billion: *IMPOSSIBLE!* It certainly is possible, and I proved it!

Just lucky, you say? I am aware of the cliché, "The harder you work, the luckier you get." There is some truth to that, but I think there is real luck that some receive. For me that comes from God and I believe most often as a result of prayer. Earl Nightingale said, "People with goals succeed because they know where they're going. It's that simple." To this very day, as I stated earlier in the book, I am thankful for stumbling across and reading about *The Strangest Secret,* along with the other books I mentioned.

They confirmed what I knew down deep. Schools and parents need to explain, teach and enable kids, especially those living in difficult situations, to set goals and the importance of networking and relationship building.

When I show people my SATs, I always remind them that my parents came to America with a fourth-grade education, so big words weren't spoken in my home.

It's my way of showing goals in action, meaning my parents wanted a better life. They were able to find their way to America, meet and get married and realize their dreams, and I was able to get into college despite having been told it was impossible!

As I have said a few times earlier, I knew we were poor, and I did not want to be poor, and I was determined not to be poor. You can tell that I seemed to know more about what I didn't want in life than what I did. Nothing wrong with that.

Keep in mind your goals can change and probably will. Many five-year-olds want to be firemen or policemen. Nothing wrong with that either.

I thought I wanted to be a teacher. I assumed that teaching meant in high school, I never contemplated that I would be teaching in business rather than high school. The original goal of being a high school teacher was actually leading me in the right direction, I just didn't know it at the time.

The point of setting goals is to allow your subconscious, in conjunction with your hard work, education, etc., to steer your efforts to success. In my previous books, I ask my readers to imagine a large cargo ship leaving port without a compass or destination. What would all the ocean currents and the waves of the North Atlantic do to its course? Where would it end up? Maybe five thousand feet at the bottom. You need a destination—a goal. Changing or fine-tuning it along the way is not a problem, and most likely will happen.

My parents were very religious and instilled

that faith in me. I prayed hard and believed in a higher power. As I said a couple of paragraphs back, my only regret is that I did not think big enough! I didn't learn till later on that a lot of well known successful people had set their goals extremely high. Again, it might sound cliché, but you can do anything you want to do, so pick something that will not only help you, but will also, and maybe even more importantly, help others. Helping others is how you become wealthy.

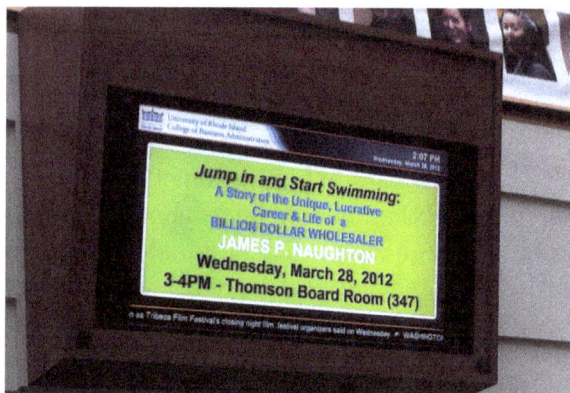

As I have said, big words were not spoken in my home, nor did I have a knack for mathematics, nor did I have a genius Einstein IQ. For my younger readers, YOU CAN ATTAIN WHATEVER YOU SET YOUR MIND TO (Google *The Strangest Secret*, by Earl Nightingale), whether it's becoming a lineman at 5'7" or getting into and graduating college with only a 754 total SAT Score. Write down what you want [a goal] then save it in a private place and let your subconscious along with hard work help steer you to your dreams.

YOU, ALSO, CAN BECOME "THE GREATEST"!

My favorite quote: "Always behave like a duck:
Keep calm and unruffled on the surface
but paddle like the devil underneath!"

~ Jacob Braude

Appendix:

*How to publish Your story as an e-book
in three easy steps*

Three easy steps to upload your story as an
E-Book on Amazon-JustPublishingAdvice.com.
If you would like some professional help, please
contact my editor Kip at *mrkipw@gmail.com*. You
can contact me as well from my website, *www.
KeyPublishingCompany.com*

My Favorite Book: *For Those I Loved,* by Martin
Gray, the author and main character. A survival
story of a young boy caught up in the German
Invasion of Poland. Each page is incredibly
suspenseful and breathtaking. It also teaches
survival. If you get a copy (it's hard to find these
days) and open to the first page, I guarantee you
won't put it down until you finish reading it. I
found a copy in 1981 and read it over several
hours at the Park Plaza Hotel fronting Central
Park, with violins playing in the background,
during High Tea. A long way from the United
Homes housing project in East Hartford!

More reminiscing of and about my classmates.
Most were children of blue collar workers, in the
factory town of Pratt and Whitney Aircraft (Now

United Technologies) East Hartford, Connecticut.

My other four books are listed here in order of publication: 1st, *Jump In and Start Swimming,* 2nd: *Relationships Open Doors,* 3rd: *Whatever Happened to the Pecords?* 4th: *Heaven Sent.*

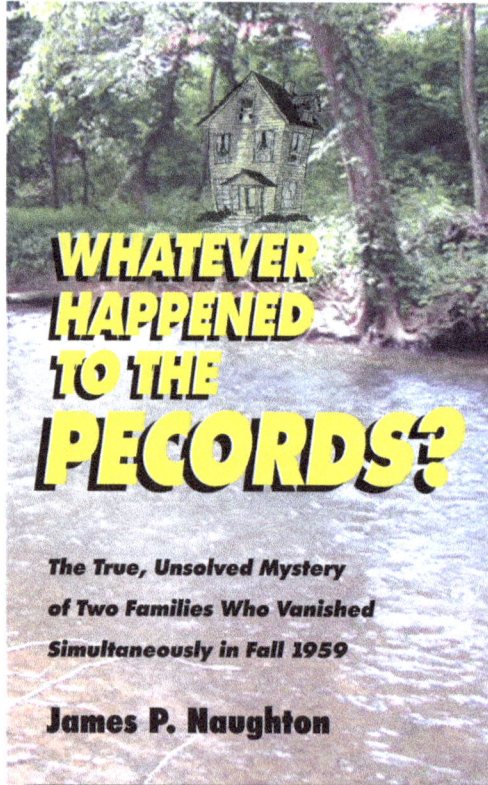

WHATEVER HAPPENED TO THE PECORDS?

The True, Unsolved Mystery of Two Families Who Vanished Simultaneously in Fall 1959

James P. Naughton

E-Book COLLEGE JOB GUIDE Amazon title: *Jump In and Start Swimming* Supplemental Guide: Job and Career Assistance for College Seniors and Recent Graduates. $1.99

ARTICLES: Woodstock Article - My 2009 East Hartford *Gazette* hometown newspaper article on my trip to Woodstock in 1969. Email me a receipt for the purchase of my books, and I will email you a copy at no charge.

WHATEVER HAPPENED TO THE PECORDS?

They were the last remote stop on the author's paper route, located 50ft from the Connecticut River. This book is a TRUE mystery of a missing family, the Pecords, who vanished from their home on a Friday evening in early fall of 1959. It is not a CRIME STORY; it may turn out to be one, but not at this time.

Parts of the theme and the era have similarities that were evident in the movie STAND BY ME which was set a year later in 1960 based on the fiction novella, "The Body" by Stephen King.

Instead of calling the police, he called two buddies to conduct their own investigation and nearly got killed. The book is also a memoir in a sense that the author allows the reader to peer into the 50's era in his hometown, by utilizing the nervous flashbacks he experienced and recorded afterward, during a run for his life. Because of a sworn oath between the author and his teenage friends, he was unable to tell his story till now.

As a coincidence, a relatively new college, Goodwin College, purchased the missing family's home and invited the author to do a tour of it, one last time. They acknowledged that they had planned to tear it down in order to build a "cottage" for hosting off-campus meetings on the site. They also shared with him how the street he grew up on got its name, Colt Street. (The missing family's home was also the last house on the street.) The fact that the house was originally part of a ferry landing set up by Samuel Colt (Colt 45) was incredible. Mr. Colt also lived at the landing while a mansion was being built for him across the street also overlooking the Connecticut River. If you log into Goodwin.com, you can maneuver a telescope on the peak of the building to view the surrounding area...webcam.goowin.edu/view/index.shtm/

Some readers have criticized that "The book was not a true crime story" and it is not, although it might be at some time in the future. Others said that "We didn't do enough investigation in regards to where the missing family might have gone". Please keep in mind that we were all age 15 at the time, roughly the same age as the kids in the movie "Stand By Me", which was set one year later in 1960. The town's police department records were destroyed 10 years later, apparently standard procedure. Later on, when we requested help from the FBI, I doubt they took us seriously. It was obviously a different era.

In discussing the story with the editor of the town newspaper, The Gazette, Bill Doakes. He informed the author, that there were a number of unsolved missing persons in town since the mid-1900's. I know it sounds implausible that these situations exist, but they do. Initially, and for a long time after the "incident", the boys kept a low profile. They were young and just plain scared that they might be implicated in a crime, especially having found a hidden wall safe's door swinging open and "empty" in the house. In fact, they agreed to never discuss it with anyone unless all three were to agree.

Please note: The search for the Pecord's is still going on primarily by the readers and classmates from East Hartford, Conn. Bits and pieces continue to flow in and will be published on the website of KeypublishingCompany.com near future. If you have something to add or questions to ask, please feel free to go to this website and press the "Contact Tab" and forward them.

Available: Amazon.com Barnes & Noble and KeyPublishingCompany.com - Book website

APPENDIX

Also part of my "How To Live Forever" Series

APPENDIX

Special Chapters for my East Hartford Classmates and Friends. *Note!* While specific to East Hartford, everyone is invited to learn about these fabulous Baby Boomer friends and classmates of mine! They are also "the Greatest"!

Additional information for my book *Whatever Happened to the Pecords?*

Note: My Pecord book advisors suggested that I remove many of the names that I had listed from my old paper route and neighborhood. I'm sorry I agreed. On Colt Street where I lived, there was Joan Trani and her sisters, Nancy and Denise, and an older sister whose name I can't recall. They played tackle football with us in seventh grade (except the youngest, Denise).

Between the Tranis and us lived Doug Sweet, a major character in *Whatever Happened to the Pecords?* A little further down lived Alan and Jackie McManus. Jack and his wife Martha live there now, in his parents home on Colt Street, which was part of my old Hartford *Times* paper route, and Donny Curtis live next door to him. RIP, Donnie, plus Joanne Chrissi on the other side.

On Crosby Street, there was Bunny Alice Bavier, who I met through Joan, and her brother Steve, and his brothers. Steve married Carol O'Brien, who lived in King Court.

At the beginning of Crosby, a block south on Main Street, lived Ugo Benneteri, brother Frank (later Willow Inn owner), and sister Connie. Theirs was a huge three-story house where we bought our Christmas Tree every year and where I tasted my first Italian food.

The Bennetieri "kids" were first generation as was I. Down towards the middle of Crosby Street was the entrance to King Court Apartments, where some of the story took place. Sandy MacDougall (recently passed on), Durwood Morin, Jeanie Boynton (about whom Sandy said, "We broke up, Norton (one of my many nicknames), so now you can date her if you want, she's going to be expensive, as I spent a lot on her!"

As I have mentioned before, in that era, I was fourteen or fifteen, going on twelve. I mean I was super naive. I didn't know what the heck he was talking about and still don't, although I recognized how cute she was. Of course, I didn't have an extra nickel then to spend on myself., let alone on a girl! Kathy Flaherty, a sweet vivacious young girl lived there; her parents were good friends with mine. Kathy did Irish step dancing with my sister Kathleen. Actually, Kathleen started her own Irish step dancing school at a young age and won many competitions here and in Ireland. Peggy O'Sullivan, Seamus' younger sister, and married to Mike Peruchio, Lenore's brother, was also in an adult class with Kathy, as was Sharon Larson Fitzgerald, Congressman John Larson's younger sister.

Donna and Irma Gregory, two gorgeous sisters, live in an upstairs apartment at the end of the circle. Babe Pelletier walked out with a ponytail and was one of the prettiest girls in the King Court complex, Barbara Fox, who was at least for a while a girlfriend of my other "Pecord" book's character, my next door neighbor, Doug Sweet. All the girls liked Doug. He was a handsome kid who had a lot more freedom than I in those years. I was kind of a goofy guy who had to be home before dark.

We—Billy White and I—were trying to locate Doug for the book signing when we learned he passed away in 2014. RIP, Doug. Carol O'Brien and her sister lived on the left side of the complex. Carol was very pretty and popular and as I mentioned married Steve Bavier. Midge Serignese, a real cutie, was my first girlfriend, sort of, for a couple of weeks at least. Donnie Munroe and the Pepins, Freddie and Joey, all part of our nightly sandlot football games; just below the entrance to King Court on the corner lived Mary Ann Dobbins, a very sweet girl where we played "ring and rung" until we got caught by her older brother.

Mary Ann married Mike Russell, an executive at the Boston firm I retired from, MFS. Can you imagine the look on my face when she showed up at my first Christmas Party at the firm in 1987 with Mike, twenty-five years after we graduated high school?

Further down on Crosby Street lived my dear friend, pretty Rachael Frechette. We first met at Bob Quesnette's birthday party.

Rachel's family and the rest on Crosby and Colt Streets were also my paper route customers. *No wonder he liked his newspaper route,* you're thinking. Yep!

Some of these kids I previously presented in the book, but I planned on naming anyone who touched my young life. So here they finally are. Forgive me if I forgot some It's been a long time.

In my era, King Court was an upscale apartment complex that contained a football field and basketball court which we made great use of back in the late '50s. Most attended Willow Brook Elementary, except for me, as I took the bus to St. Mary's in the North End. So in a way it was a bit awkward for me: I moved to the neighborhood not knowing anyone, and I attended a different school on the opposite end of town. I heard, but haven't confirmed that Goodwin College/University purchased the King Court Apartment Complex.

Speaking of Willow Brook, one of my best friends in that period along with Billy White was Ricky Dickman. I borrowed our high-school prom picture from the Pecords book, as Ricky is also a main character in it, and placed it below. So these are most of the kids, some of whose names were removed from this book's first draft.

It was exciting magical time in our lives, accented with the best "doo wop" oldie songs, and I miss it all. "Sherry Baby... won't you come out tonght?" (Franki Valli) Please read *Whatever Happened to the Pecords?* especially if you want to remember that time. My book website is *www. KeyPublishingCompany.com*

Ricky Dickman (right) and the author in "A White Sport Coat and a Pink Carnation" all dressed up for our prom 1962 [Song by Marty Robbins, 1957], borrowed from Whatever Happened to the Pecords?

APPENDIX

More on my book *Whatever Happened to the Pecords?* and more East Hartford stuff.

Thanks to all who attended:

My college book signing for *Whatever Happened to the Pecords?* on October 16, 2014, was sponsored by Goodwin College, East Hartford,

Connecticut. (NOTE: Goodwin recently became a university). The college purchased the home that originally belonged to the missing Pecord family on the banks of the Connecticut River.

Vice President Todd Andrews approved the event for me at the college. Coincidentally, his assistant was Maura Callahan. She is also the daughter of my St. Mary's friend and classmate, Geoff Callahan. Geoff was a little older in our St. Mary's 9th grade class, and he ended up driving me, Jimmy Maloney, Franki Grandi, and some girls, to our class outing at Ocean Beach Park, New London, CT. Sadly Geoff passed away not too long after attending the signing. I am grateful for the opportunity to meet his wife Gloria for the first time, and another daughter, Mary Ellen.

While touring the college before the event, Todd Andrews informed me that Goodwin had just purchased Gilo's, a pub on Main Street owned by my St. Mary's classmate Frankie Grandi, who he immediately dialed and put me on speaker phone with. Frankie, who'd just gotten a windfall buyout, was walking down the street at Saratoga Race Track with George Raymond. *Can't make this stuff up!*

I mean... Funny! "Frankie?" "Norti, what's going on?" I said "You finally sold your place for ten times what it was worth, and you're giving it to the horses?" We both started laughing. (You need to read about our crazy antics at St. Mary's in my *Whatever Happened to the Pecords?* George and his brother David Raymond were also St. Mary's alumni. I hung around with both of them back then.

When you read the chapter discussing my career as a power lineman at HELCO and learn how their older brother Donnie, who I had never known even existed, took me under his wing when I first started out, you may get the impression that a higher power was watching over me. Plus, five years later, after basically no contact, all three brothers showed up unexpectedly at my stag party. Unreal! Note again, that I mention many times—probably too many—that I don't believe in coincidences, but I write about tons of them. As I have also said, it's just an easy way to explain the unseen hand of God.

The turnout for my book signing was fantastic. We had close to 150 guests. Thanks to Goodwin and Todd Andrews for placing an ad in the Hartford *Courant*, the state's largest newspaper at the time. What was really touching for me was the number of "kids" like Geoff, whom I had attended St. Mary's with, that came that night, some going back to Kindergarten. Unreal! St. Mary's was more than a school; it was family. Jimmy Boldstrich, Katie McLaughlan (RIP, Katie), Nicky Guidice, Tony Roberto, and Bonnie Filmore and I would meet up at the nostalgic Eastwood Theater for the Saturday matinee when we were in eighth grade.

In addition to my wife, Sharon, my children, Tim and wife Cristina, Matt and daughter Erin, of course my sister Kathy, champion Irish step dancer and former owner of The Kathleen

Naughton Connolly Irish Step Dancing School, and
husband Mike Connolly (RIP, Mike). Their children,
my nieces and nephews: Mike Jr., and wife Toula
Colonel Sean Connolly and wife Carol all attended,
as did John and Marti Driscoll Choquette. I
immediately put them all on my iPhone with
Jimmy Maloney living in Dallas, Texas. It was like
a mini grammar school reunion before my book
signing event commenced.

After the call, I turned around and there
was Lenore Perucchio Jordan and Peggy Deleo,
both of whom were also classmates from St.
Mary's. (As I am writing this, I'm sad to hear that
Peggy's younger brother, Jimmy, also a St. Mary's
alumnus, passed on. RIP, Jimmy. God bless you).
Lenore married my friend Jimmy Jordan (see
Jerry Ceniglio's wedding picture in the beginning).
Lenore and Peggy were among the nicest girls at
St. Mary's. Thinking about it, everyone there was
the best. They are family. Again, sadly, as I finished
this book I was informed that another St. Mary's
classmate, Judy Kiro, passed. Judy was a sweet,
pretty girl from the class behind mine. RIP, Judy.

I was also glad to see Ernie Hutt, owner of
our famous Augie and Ray's drive-in restaurant,
which is prominently mentioned and displayed
in my *Whatever Happened to the Pecords?* Ernie
ended up selling my book at Augie's, generously
providing his ever-.popular hot dogs as a freebie
to book buyers! Unknown to me at the time, Ernie
was also selling a book *Stories From The Fifties,
East Hartford Style,* by Jack Laplante, famous East
Hartford Athlete, Hartford High school teacher.

and football coach, whom I have yet to meet.

Jack is friends with Jim Maloney's brother, Dick Maloney, as well as Jack Sullivan, all from a few classes before ours. Of course, my Central Connecticut Veteran's Club buddies, Tommy Connolly, Ronnie Perham, "The Captain," and Eddy Satalino (as mentioned earlier, a star football player from our East Hartford High era) showed up to support me.

Bill Humphreys, who began with the Class of '62, but left for prep school, stopped in. He became an international bicyclist who was in the midst of selling his own book *The Jersey Project.* His sister Amber and I met at the Aircraft Credit Union where we both worked part-time during high school. Frank Raffa, who inherited and ran his family's package store, also came by.

Jerry Ceniglio and I also reunited at the event. It had been a while since we met up in the Merrill Lynch building in New Haven while we were both still working in 2006.

Finally, my St. Mary's classmate Nicky Guidice showed up, and I signed his copy of my book. We met in fifth grade when Nicky moved to East Hartford from Lynne, Massachusetts. Nicky was a great varsity wrestler back in the day.

The morning after the book signing, my wife Sharon was watching Good Morning America and noted that their guest was the famous author, James Patterson, who was lamenting that he only had six people show up for his recent book signing. So, no question: My Goodwin College book signing event, with approximately 150 in attendance, was successful.

Unbelievable! Speaking of books and just now I'm listening to, "I wonder, wonder... who? Who wrote the Book of Love?" (The Monotones, 1958—their only hit, but a great one!) Here is how my generation's music has helped my memories. It's not just me, I heard a 64-year-old Buddy Holly oldie in a TV commercial yesterday. That's right—64 years old! Our music was/is magical: No question.

I was delivering papers on Crosby Street in the summer of '58. This kid and his friends are approaching, carrying a transistor radio. The song playing was "Book of Love." Hadn't heard it before, but I knew I liked the song. I didn't like the fact that one of the kids' buddies shoved him up against my bike, knocking over my paper bag! It was done intentionally to instigate a situation. I didn't know a lot of kids then. As I mentioned, I took a bus north to St. Mary's and almost everyone in my area went to Willowbrook Grammar school.

The kid said to his older friends "he can probably kick my butt," knowing full well he believed he could kick mine, and he probably would have as I never learned to back down. Fortunately, another kid whom I had recently met through Billy White, Bobby Lockwood, pulled up on his bicycle. Bobby, who was a little older and very mature for his age, lived out on Main Street in front of the kid's house, and he proceeded to introduce us.

The kid's name was Ricky Dickman. Ricky, sensing my interest, handed me his radio to look over. In an instant, everything was smoothed over, and Ricky and I became close friends. *He was the best kid!* By the way, Ricky became a varsity football player. He was a well-built, strong, tough kid. Not a brawler, but you would not have wanted to tangle with him. Whew! Thanks, Bobby Lockwood wherever you are!! You can read more about him in my book *Whatever Happened to the Pecords?*

Some additional remembrances of my East Hartford classmates and friends as previously described.

After the publication and the Goodwin College book signing event for *Whatever Happened to the Pecords?* I continue to hear from many of my former friends and classmates.

I reunited by email with my home room friend (from Mr.Harvey's class), a lovely girl with stunning long black hair, Carol Leone Baldwin, who I used to walk to our first class with, and I learned that she married, raised a family and became a Senior Vice President for Disney World in Orlando.

As I previously mentioned, a classmate located our high school English teacher, Leonard Engel, now a professor at Quinnipiac college. It was Carol, and she facilitated our reunion. Sandy Stanizzi married Joe Pezzente (Sandy was a St.

Mary's classmate), who also sat in front of me in Mr. Harvey's Home room, always telling a quick joke or singing songs like "Lollipop, lollipop, ooh lolly, lolly, lolly..." (The Chordettes, 1958—I mean who remembers this stuff? Me!)

Between these happenstance internet meetings and our Class Reunions, we slowly begin to find out what everyone has been doing over the years.

"What they've been doing" is part of our Baby Boomer generation experience. In 2017, at our 50th reunion, I met Leah Witkowski Mangiafico. I think I last saw her at the Blue Sands in Misquamicut in '63. I think we were allowed in to dance only with a stamp, as we weren't yet 21. She looked terrific then, and terrific as a wife, a mother and a grandmother at our 50th class reunion.

I also reunited with Marti Sincere, my sister's former Bunco player, at an East Hartford town reunion in Venice Beach, FL, 2015—unfortunately, the last one. Great gal, spirited personality and very attractive. I still correspond on Facebook with Donna Malon Vanasse, also from St. Mary's.

Donna was and is a sweetheart, and a grandmother many times. It seems that now our early school lives and acquaintanceships are coming full circle.

I worked with Dianne Fournier and others for our 55th, 2017 Class Reunion. Dianne remembers me talking about a missing family that I was going to write about during our senior year; *Whatever*

Happened to the Pecords?, was published in 2013, 51 years later! The 55th reunion was held at her and her husband's Glastonbury Country Club. Dianne is still as attractive as she was in high school.

Many attended, including Elaine Keeney who I haven't seen since graduation in 1962. She looked the same—terrific! Always a great kid. Vinny Knapp, his wife Lynn and associates provided our entertainment and were awesome. Many remembered Vinny from high school when he was the drummer for the Nocturnes.

Note: The next few paragraphs are also dedicated to my friends in my hometown, East Hartford, CT. As mentioned, this book has many intentions. Since it is a memoir, I wanted to acknowledge the "kids" that touched my life even in a small way early on. I was gifted with great long-term memory, so I am leaving a sentence or two of my recollections of them.

RIP, Frank Raffa, who owned Raffa's Package Store. A great guy! My friends and I helped him expand his business, probably a little too much. Frank was in our class, 1962.

RIP, Ann Spencer. My mother and her mother always wanted us to go out while we were attending St. Mary's. Of course, she was Irish, but that had nothing to do with it, right? I was her dance partner during 9th grade, but that was as far as it got. I never got to use the Fox Trot with her, or anyone.

Maybe stepping all over her feet was the problem. She told me when we met at our 55th class Reunion planning event that she married the best guy. I was happy for her. A sweet girl, who recently passed on this past year. RIP, Ann.

RIP, Ricky Dickman, who I just wrote about, a few paragraphs back; my childhood friend and a main character in my book *Whatever Happened to the Pecords?* left us in his mid thirties, way too young! I placed a picture of us in the previous chapter. Sadly, I was living in Rhode Island when I heard, a month after his passing, and missed his service. On top of that, his mom passed away a week later, so I missed both; terrible, but it's really only since the late 80s that we have such advanced communications where we hear of news quickly, instantly. My company gave me my first cell phone in 1991, a Panasonic the size of a shoe box when taken out—installed in my car for $2500.

Lee McNamara drove us to the Junior Prom and was a great fisherman... Well, he liked to fish. His sister Cynthia, a class or two behind us, helped me in my attempt to find Pecord family members after reading my book. You can find some of her work on my book website *www. KeyPublishingCompany.com* I went with pretty Betty Doyle Zizzamia, a super nice gal.

I asked Dianne Rivers, a cute sophomore, to our Senior Prom, and I admit I was a complete immature jerk. It seemed as though I was more interested in the guys at the beach party the next day. *No, not that way,* it's just that I was so glad to be done with high school and trying to figure out what to do. I spent a lot of time listening to what others were going to do, completely unnecessary. Many of my friends were joining the Navy Reserve; as I stated, I didn't have any real close friends going on to college. So you can see a young girl having her feelings hurt, especially being around an older group of seniors. I have regretted it ever since. I don't like hurting people and wouldn't intentionally, unless they were trying to hurt me. If she was my daughter, I would have kicked my a$$!

Soon after graduation, I was supposed to meet Tony Micheletti and a few others in Old Saybrook at Jimmy Lynch's parents' summer cottage. The plan was to take a rowboat and go out swimming off the Point. I had gone on the weekend before, but something came up, and I had to cancel.

Jimmy tragically dove off the boat in about four feet of water, and his head struck a rock. He was permanently paralyzed from his neck down, for the rest of his life. It's one of the reasons that my pool does not have a diving board and is seven feet in the deep end instead of eight. It's designated as a non-diving pool.

This was awful, a catastrophe, the worst. At seventeen or eighteen, it's nearly impossible to fully comprehend. Even now, 58 years later, I start to hyperventilate, thinking of what happened to him and what possibly could have happened to me, in an instant! It tells us to be careful, while stressing how fragile our lives are. Coincidentally, a similar incident and resulting paralysis occurred with a classmate of my son's around their high-school graduation here in Rhode Island.

Unfortunately, these accidents happen, and it seems that they often occur in the period around and following one's Senior year, particularly with young guys feeling so good and invincible in life. "Nothing can take them (us) down!" We have all felt indestructible. No young person can picture being taken so young. It's almost impossible to think so. I hesitate to even mention this horrific event, but if it can prevent another accident, so be it.

Also, RIP, Esther Buffington. She left us recently. She was so pleasant and awesome to be around, and helpful in our planning of the 55th reunion. I worked with her older brother Clark, and also with Denny Tillotson's sister Dianne at the Credit Union.

Steve Bavier from my old neighborhood (I've mentioned that his parents were newspaper customers of mine on Crosby Street) passed on very young. His friend Sandy McDougal, whom I mentioned earlier from around the corner in King Court, Class of '61, also passed last year. RIP, Steve and Sandy.

Also, St. Mary's own "Annette Funicello," Geraldine Giuelli Lerz, passed away after a long illness. It was very sad to learn of her long-suffering. I have known her since second grade. Her husband Ronnie Lerz, Class of '61, passed on soon after. RIP, Geraldine and Ronnie.

Also, RIP Carol McClain, who I took to our St. Mary's ninth grade Senior Prom, a nice, sweet girl. My sister remains close friends with Carol's younger sister Gayle.

Dorothy Montano came to our 50th class reunion. She looked terrific. We attended St. Mary's also, way back in second or third grade. Her brother Rocco owned a gas station in East Hartford, and was in my sister Kathleen's Class of '63. Rocco was also a St, Mary's alum. RIP, Rocco.

Speaking of third grade, many will remember Rose Lynch, one of the few teachers who were not nuns. I was with Jane and her brother Joseph Lynch with their mother, Rose Lynch, as our teacher in third grade. I haven't heard from either one since '62 and hope that they are both doing well. Jane had the best ninth-grade parties at her big white house on Main Street, just up the road from St. Mary's. I occasionally hear from Anthony Roberto, a St. Mary's alumnus, along with John Abetz . Skip Akerlund often attended the reunions with Ronnie Perham.

I continued thinking some more of 1963 and my East Hartford friends as I continued toward the Cape.

I hung around with Tony Marchese, a handsome blonde-haired, blue-eyed Italian kid, also Class of '62. Tony was waiting to get into a state technical college while I was trying to figure what I wanted to do.

Everyone liked Tony, guys and girls. He was

just one of those kids. He had something special in his personality. Other than Tony, I didn't have any close friends that went to college after graduating high school.

Tony introduced me to Neldy Noel from his neighborhood, and we hung out that summer. Tony was also friends with musician Billy Durso, and knowing I liked the music, he introduced us. Billy was the self-taught guitarist for our high school band the Nocturnes, I thought he did the best rendition of "What I'd Say?"—as good as Ray Charles, for my money, and this was high school.

If you didn't go to college after high school it felt that you were, in a way, marking time, waiting to turn 21. We were old enough to go to war but not old enough to get into clubs. Fortunately we all met up at a Nocturnes reunion dance at the Marco Polo, mid-'90s

Tony and I found ourselves attending the Class of '63 high school fraternity and sorority dances, with the Nocturnes, that were formerly held at Italian American Club, now at the I.A.M. Union, all on South Main Street.

We also became friends with Nocturnes drummer Vinny Knapp, and I still meet up occasionally to hear Vinny and his wife Lynne perform. They get better with the years. I mentioned that they provided terrific entertainment at our 55th class reunion in October, 2017. You've got to watch for their shows and take one in. They are currently appearing at the Flying Monkey, Berlin Turnpike, Newington, Connecticut.

Tony Marchese and I became what I called "band groupies" and went with them to U CONN Fraternity dances. As a result we also became friends with the guys from the class of '63, Pete Bengsten, Terry Hobby, Gregg Hopkins, and the girls. Debbie Hopkins, Gregg's younger sister, was a cutie whom everyone liked. Mary Hutt was a sweet girl and sister of my friend Ernie Hutt, owner of Augie and Ray's, and a bookseller. So many great kids I can see in my mind's eye, but age is causing me to forget names. God bless them all.

Pete Bengston passed away a while ago, on October 1, 2004, and Gregg Hopkins did also last year. RIP, Pete and Gregg. You are missed by all. Every once in a while I speak with Pat Dwyer, an attorney in Glastonbury. Pat was Class President for the Class of 1963. He attended St. Mary's for eight years with me, in the class behind.

His assistant was Patti Geci, a real nice kid. I heard she remarried and moved to Colorado. I remember and think fondly of Regina Moriarty, a beautiful girl whom I last met coming back from her cross country trip to San Francisco, and Joanne Barry, who came to one of our crazy Veteran Club dances. Both terrific, great girls. I hope life has been good to them. They deserved the best, as do all of my East Hartford friends.

More thoughts on East Hartford classmates and fellow Baby Boomers. "The Loco-Motion"

(Little Eva, 1962) is playing on the Cape Cod oldie station: "Everybody's doin' a brand new dance now..."

Johnny Barone and Seamus O'Sullivan would pick me and Tony up on Sundays, and we would drive to Brewster, NY. We made the most of what many of us considered a boring period, waiting to turn 21. Both have passed on. RIP, Johnny and Seamus. In that period I was also friends with Teddy Lata. In fact, I can still see him cruising on Burnside Ave with his green Pontiac Convertible, it seemed like it was a whole city block long. They don't make them like that anymore.

Teddy was with Tony Micheletti whom he called "Meats" and also Bobby Lombardo. These guys were part of the Class of '63. I know Teddy started a painting business. However, I haven't seen any of them since that time.

During the 80s and part of the 90s, as I was returning from New York State or other parts of my large territory, I would drive through East Hartford, and occasionally I would see guys from high school, like Bruce Ryalls standing outside the fire station on Main Street. I'm not saying we were the closest friends, it's just that regardless of where I went and no matter how supposedly great I succeeded in business. I have never forgotten my roots or my East Hartford friends. My stories not only give me a hobby, they give me a chance to think back and relive, for better or worse—mostly for the better—events, friends and relationships that I believe will provide my readers with some entertainment, and possibly offer some life and business ideas for their children and grandchildren, and of course, my own.

I would purposefully stop at Wayne Lerz's barber shop in the South End to get a haircut plus catch up on all the East Hartford news, plus listen to Wayne belt out a couple of Frank Sinatra songs. Wayne turned out to be a good singer and stand up comedian and mimic. Often, Leo Bruculio and Benny Romano would be hanging out in Wayne's shop. That's how I kept in touch during the pre-computer, pre-cell phone era.

RIP, Johnny Watson, who passed this year. He was a part of my Willow Inn Campus when he was not driving his semi. His friend Bobby Campman, a fun, crazy kid, went one on one at the Willow Inn with John Hollis, half John's size. Didn't win, but big b@##s! ...and a little crazy, in a fun way. He also passed a while back. RIP, Bobby.

I used to think in those days, "I wouldn't want to be a stranger walking into the Willow for the first time and knowing no one." It was my college campus, but it could be dangerous to a stranger.

I mentioned this before, but I heard recently that a character in the Apple TV miniseries "Defending Jacob" referred to East Hartford as, "one tough town." It was! Hopefully, more on this later if I hear anything. I also was told that Kenny Grant was given his freedom. I remember him as a funny, likable kid back in high school, when he and Jimmy Maloney let the huge snapping turtle out in the hallway and then pulled the alarm. I hope he has found peace.

Bobby and Herby Elliot and many others, especially from the South End, are fading in my mind. We would bump into them at Big Jim's, the other South End Pratt and Whitney pub. Once in a while we would all meet up at the Yankee, next door to Big Jim's. When I said that there were lots of bars in the South End, I meant it.

People worked hard in the P&W plant, often without air conditioning, and they need a place to cool off. East Hartford was a "tough" factory town.

Every so often I would meet with high school sons of the Willow's customers and help them pick courses for the coming semester, and also tutor them with courses they were having difficulty with.

I know it sounds crazy, but that's the way it was. It wasn't Beverly Hills, it was East Hartford, in the early to mid sixties!

I previously mentioned that we attended an East Hartford town reunion at the Venice Country Club in Venice, Florida, in February, 2015. I can't recall everyone, but Lester Hope was there, as were Leah Witkowski Mangiafico with her younger sister, along with Marti Sincere, John and Marti Choquette, Jim and Dick Maloney, my sister Kathleen, and brother-in-law Mike Connolly.

Johnny White was also there. He has been living next door in Englewood for quite some time. As it turned out there was a significant group of folks from East Hartford who retired to Englewood, FL.

Later that evening, a bunch of us met up with Jack Sullivan and his wife afterward at the Englewood Elks Club and enjoyed listening to a great oldie band.

Dick Maloney, Jim's brother, accompanied us and was, at the time, President and Exalted Ruler of the Jacksonville, Florida, Elks Lodge, so we had no problem getting in and had a terrific dinner for only about $10.00. Drinks were about a quarter of the normal price. Great time! Great oldie band!

It seemed that a number of former East Hartford firemen retired to the area also. I do recall Doug and Barbara Danahy at the Venice Country Club, high school sweethearts from our Class of '62. I had lost track of Doug since high school and was proud when I heard he had joined the US Marines and served in Vietnam. Sadly, Doug passed on earlier this year. RIP, Doug: Semper Fi!

I have lost track of Tommy Hickey. I also got him a part-time job at the Auto Club during college. Tommy passed away recently, as did Johnny Paolino. RIP, Johnny and Tommy.

I missed our first class reunion in '67, but came to the new Sonesta Hotel, at Constitution Plaza, to attend the second, in 1972, with my wife, Sharon, whom I married in '71.

I remember asking for Tony Marchese and

someone said he passed. *What?* I couldn't believe it. I couldn't get a full story—another said he was born with a congenital heart defect. He never told me that. Tony and I lost our connection after I went into the Marines. No argument, things just change when you're young and sometimes fast. For some reason when thinking of Tony, I remember Cynthia Brown, Class 63, (I think), a nice kid, and attractive.

I also believe Tony was good friends with Pam Dunphy from our class, she was very nice... stunning, actually!

I heard he started engineering college. Even now I am looking for answers. I did locate a recent obituary for his older brother, Richard Marchese, and there was a mention of "Uncle Tony."

I also inquired numerous times about the whereabouts of Bill Carbone, forgetting that he might have been class of '61(not sure about that) and was told he suddenly moved to Florida to be near family. I was never able to reach him. I wish him well. Great guy! The best!

These "kids" were all part of a magical era and are along with myself, referred to as Baby Boomers who touched my life in some way. So it's an honor to acknowledge them in my "How To Live Forever" book series!

Finally, I wish to leave a special tribute to those East Hartford friends and classmates who made the ultimate sacrifice during the Vietnam Conflict. I mentioned Bobby Beamon, USMC,

Mayberry Village, from my platoon earlier, killed in an amphibious landing on a Vietnam beach. In my Woodstock article, I mentioned Captain Fran Sullivan, who died there. He was a couple of classes ahead of mine.

Most recently, I learned that my high school friend Martha Sincere's younger brother, James Sincere, USMC, was killed in Vietnam along with 50,000 other young men and women. I thank them and ask God to bless them and their families. RIP, and Semper Fi!

Vietnam was our Baby Boomer war, or conflict, and it still affects our lives in many, many ways.

My St. Mary's classmate, Johnny Armstrong, a small kid, tough as nails, was chosen to be a "tunnel rat." His job was to crawl into snake-infested, booby-trapped Viet Cong tunnels with a bayonet held between his teeth, a grenade and a .45 in his hands to capture Viet Cong. They tied a rope to his leg in case they had to pull him back out quickly. I know people who couldn't stay in a dark room for more than five minutes, so you get the picture. I also believe that none of you reading this would want your son or daughter or grandchildren to be "tunnel rats." Neither did Johnny's!

Since this is the last in my series "How to Live Forever," I'm hopeful my readers, especially the younger ones who maybe are not living in ideal circumstances and trying to find their way, can relate to the underlying theme of "you can achieve anything you set your mind to."

It doesn't matter about your present circumstances or how smart you are. Two of my wealthiest friends have never gone to college. In fact, one didn't graduate high school.

I would also like to point out that everyone has their own personal measure of what success is for them. For many it's a large house and an expensive car, along with a significant bank account.

I can tell you again from my many years of personal and business experience, including good times and not-so-good times, that your best success might be measured in how you treat everyone, especially "the least of your brethren"! For me, my best success has come from my family and the love and respect we have for one another.

SO HERE IS MY SUCCESS

My wife Sharon, my daughter Erin, sons Matthew and Timothy and Tim's wife and our daughter-in- law Cristina and their children- our grandsons -Jack, Sam and Cole

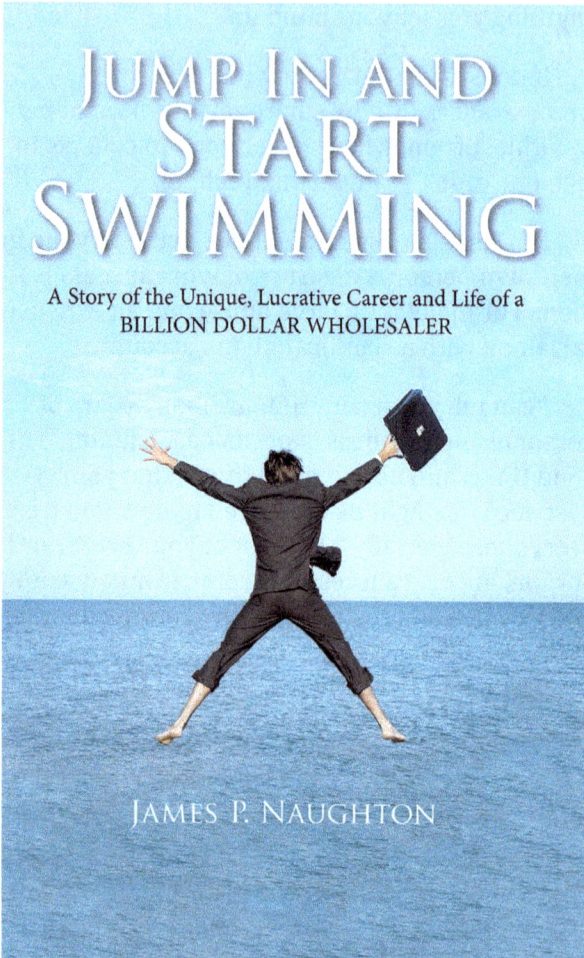

JUMP IN AND START SWIMMING

A Story of the Unique, Lucrative Career and Life of a
BILLION DOLLAR WHOLESALER

JAMES P. NAUGHTON

As I said earlier, "Students need to learn the skills of relationship building and networking in order to find a job and to advance in business and life!"

JUMP IN AND START SWIMMING

JUMP IN AND START SWIMMING was written as a result of a request by a friend and adjunct professor at the   University of Rhode Island to speak to his junior and senior students, who were beginning to find it difficult to secure jobs/careers after graduation. He knew that I had a myriad of jobs and experiences including, Restaurants, Banking/Credit Union, Electric Power Lineman, Construction, Insurance and Wall Street and more.

The 2009 Stock Market Crash accelerated and Economic Crash that decimated the job market. He believed that with all my experience, I could provide a "spark" to help them with their search. I agreed to write a "talk" to be submitted to the dean of Business, however, I found myself writing way beyond plans. When I finally called the professor to schedule coming on campus to give my "talk", I was informed of "How much worse the job situation had become since we first spoke". I also learned that a number of students' parents had unfortunately been laid off and were about to face the difficulty of paying for student loans, especially unnerving, since their kids weren't finding jobs after four years in college. It was becoming a serious mess with no end in sight. In fact all three of my grown children had lost their jobs in what was beginning to look like the 2nd Great Depression. At the time I was initially invited in to speak, I had already begun to write a memoir describing my unique careers along with some family history for my grandchildren.

My parents landed on Ellis Island in a fiercely cold winter during The Great Depression with just the clothes on their backs. I knew their story of course and I was aware of how they survived. With, No Money! No Jobs! No Unemployment! No Social Security! No place to live! No Nothing! So I thought to share their story along with discussing my career information, I might inspire the students to "press on" by including real life struggles and overcoming obstacles during what was an even scarier time in American History, while introducing them to new career opportunities.

The combination of the two caused my "talk" to evolve into a book. I just needed a title. I decided on a saying that my mother often quoted, "Jump in and Start Swimming". It was her way of telling us to take a leap of faith, when she saw us stuck or unable to make a decision. As you will learn upon reading my stories, her saying had a profound effect on my life. Once my readers,mostly students, finished the book, they emailed me, requesting more information about, "How I did, what I did?" To accommodate their requests, I wrote "RELATIONSHIPS OPEN DOORS", which describes the number one technique that I employed for over 30 years. The art of building relationships and networking is..... "A SKILL THAT EVERY COLLEGE STUDENT WILL NEED TO LEARN IN ORDER TO SECURE A CAREER!"
        This book is also, one example of allowing a part of my life to "LIVE ON FOREVER". My great, great, great grandchildren will be able to locate it on line.

Order from Amazon.com or KeyPublishingCompany.com (My book website)

We are all surrounded by negativity, so I learned to keep repeating positive affirmations,

"If it's meant to be, it's up to me."

"There is Gold Dust in the air and it's coming to me now!"

Close your eyes and imagine seeing this. Write down your goals and file them in the drawer. Get positive thinking books and read a little daily. Then silently pray to God, your Father. Take a breath, and pause and listen to your vast innermost self. I believe you will be successful and so should you.

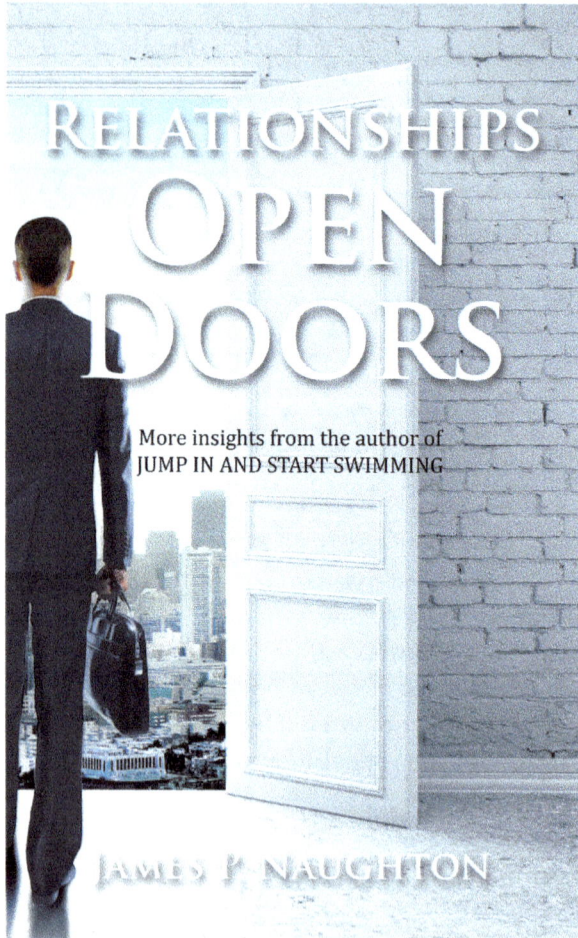

Thank you for reading this and my other books, Jump In and Start Swimming, Relationships Open Doors, Heaven Sent, Whatever Happened to the Pecords?, plus the college

job guide and the Woodstock article. You should now be ready to:

RELATIONSHIPS OPEN DOORS

"RELATIONSHIPS OPEN DOORS" is a sequel to the author's first book "Jump in and Start Swimming", which was written to help college students get jobs during the recent recession. Students and parents who read his first book and attended his "talks" during his day at URI, requested Mr. Naughton to elaborate on what techniques he employed to obtain a career(s) and then become extremely successful in those careers.

This book contains valuable information on his most important techniques, building relationships and networking. It is a skill that EVERY COLLEGE STUDENT WILL NEED TO MASTER IN ORDER TO OBTAIN A CAREER!! It is written in textbook fashion with several takeaways at the end of each chapter.

Sage advice for all new Sales/Marketing trainees to help jumpstart their careers. The author allows you the reader a window to watch and learn, as he takes you back with him more than 30 years to the beginning. This is not a book based on theory, but rather a step by step guide to show you how he learned and developed the important skill of "relationship building".

He suggests you read JUMP IN AND START SWIMMING first, followed by this sequel. This a self help book and also part of the LIVE Forever series as its based on his life and business career.

Only $2.99 as an ebook on Kindle, Amazon.com or Nook, BarnesNoble.com ($6.99 paperback)

JUMP IN AND START SWIMMING!—and write down your or your family's story!

NOTE: As I have previously mentioned, you don't have to write a book, a couple or more pages might be enough. I am a professional storyteller, so my stories tend to be longer, just as I outlined a friend's personal story at the beginning of this book.

Please feel free to log on to my book site at *www.KeyPublishingCompany.com* and check out my newspaper story of what I refer to as my Forrest Gump trip to Woodstock in 1969. There you will also find a short, but riveting, story of my family's Christmas miracle in 1949. Both are examples of very short stories that might trigger ideas for your own. If you need advice or help contact me via my website (see above).

James P Naughton

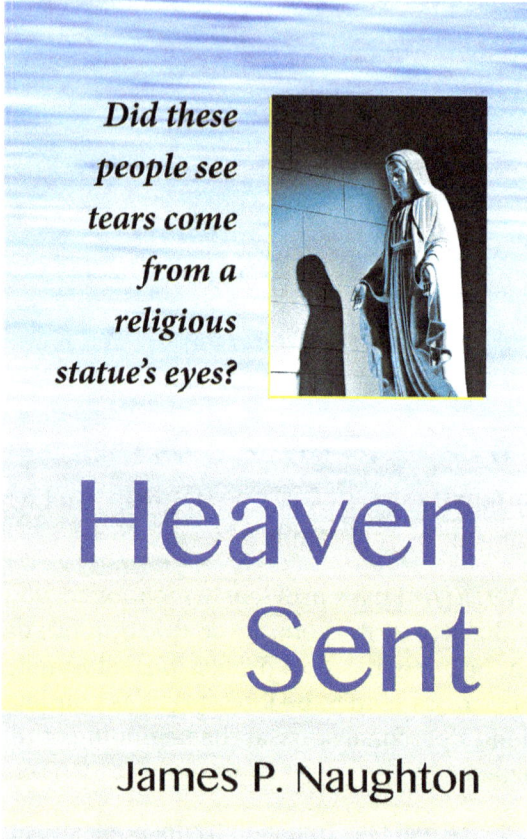

Did these people see tears come from a religious statue's eyes?

Heaven Sent

James P. Naughton

This book is intended to inform visitors to Hobbs, New Mexico of what they may encounter at Our Lady of Guadeloupe Church.

Based on the author and his family's own personal experience with a crying statue of Mother Mary in Virginia, 1992.

Partial Listing of Mother Mary's Apparitions *(from page 23)*

Our Lady of Alotting, Germany 660
Our Lady of Loreto, Italy 1291
Our Lady of Siauliai, Lithuania 1457
Our Lady of Good Counsel, Genazzano, Italy . 1467
Our Lady of Guadalupe, Mexico 1531
Our Lady of Ocotlan, Mexico 1541
Our Lady of Czestochowa, Poland 1655
Our Lady of Laus, France 1664
Our Lady of Peace, Santa Fe, New Mexico . . . 1680
Our Lady of the Miraculous Medal,
  Rue du Bac, Paris, France 1830
Our Lady of La Salette, France 1846
Our Lady of Lourdes, France 1858
Our Lady of Pontmain, France 1871
Our Lady of Knock, Ireland 1879
Our Lady of Pompeii (Our Lady of the Rosary)
  1884
Our Lady of Fatima, Portugal 1916
Our Lady of Beauraing, Belgium 1932
Our Lady of Banneux, Belgium 1933
Our Lady of Tears, Syracuse, Italy 1953
Our Lady of Akita, Japan 1973
Our Lady of Medjugorje 1981
Our Lady of Kibeho, Africa. 1981
Our Lady of the Redeemer, Bloomington, Indiana
  1990
Our Lady of the Rosary of San Nicolas,
  Buenos Aires, Argentina 1983–1990
Mary Apparitions in Tensta, Sweden 2012

Postscript: September 24, 2021

I have always told stories since I was a kid. After retiring and after the subsequent economic crash, a friend, retired CEO and an Adjunct Professor at URI, who I met at a wedding in California, asked if I would come in and speak to his Junior and Senior classes on my various jobs and careers. He knew I'd had quite a few! The idea was to create a "spark" and help students who after four years of college weren't finding jobs. That was it. I said OK, but I never heard about it again.

A few months later Mark called and asked "When are you coming in?" I said "You tell me!" He said the situation had gotten worse with the kids not getting job offers. He said "The Dean of Business wants to be involved and would like a copy of your talk." *Oh great, what am I getting myself into?* I thought.

I was, at the time, writing a memoir for my grandchildren of my various jobs and careers, plus how my parents had landed on Ellis Island in the coldest winter in the height of The Great Depression. The fact that my parents survived and went on to a better life showed survival, goals, things they probably never knew that they possessed. So I ended up taking my talk and my memoir and merging them.

When Mark called a third time I told him that my talk was evolving into a book. He said finish it and they'd buy it. He noted that the kids' parents were now getting laid off and couldn't afford the student loans for their kids, who couldn't get jobs! Many have already forgotten what a disastrous time it was for the country.

I titled the book/story (I like "story" because that's what I do, as opposed to calling it a literary work of art. I tell and write true stories.) *Jump In and Start Swimming,* after a quote my Irish mother would shout when she saw us procrastinating.

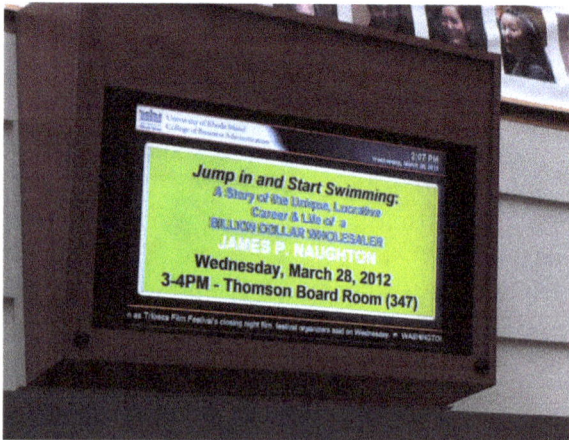

This is what all twenty of the campus marquees were flashing when I arrived. Could you ever imagine what was going through my mind? *I grew up as a first-generation American, living in a former military project during my early years, and*

rather poor. We didn't get our first family car until my junior year. Almost dropped out of high school. Had terrible SATs and was told to forget about college. "It wasn't possible."

That morning, Dean Higgins of the Business Department handed me a key to his classroom and said, "They're all yours, Jim"—all eighty of them! What I did for the next hour could be another small book. I held three large sessions in the student center, plus a series of one-on-ones throughout the day.

At the request of students, I wrote *Relationships Open Doors,* believing that while they asked for a lot of additional information, relationships and networking were, in my view, two of the most important steps for them to take and learn about. I also wrote a rudimentary College Job Guide, just to have "something to work off of."

Afterwards, I actually spent about a year discussing jobs, careers and life with many of the students at no charge. I couldn't bring myself to charge them, in light of the circumstances. The school did buy a lot of my books.

It sounds crazy and I won't get into it here, but a new college, Goodwin College, in my hometown and near my old street, ended up sponsoring a childhood story I had been writing for over fifty years: *Whatever Happened to the Pecords?*

A high-school classmate located my 11th-grade English teacher who made me stay in

high school, Leonard Engle. I had quit to join the
Marines with many of my neighborhood buddies.
He might have saved my life.

We met in 2015, at Quinnipiac University,
Hamden, CT, where he was the senior English
Professor. He insisted we start off in the oldest
and largest Irish Famine living museum in the US
in Hamden, and operated by Quinnipiac. We spent
almost a full day together and exchanged books.
His was two and a half inches thick—a treatise on
Clint Eastwood, of all topics—and mine, about the
Pecords, was about half an inch!

I followed it with *Heaven Sent.* It describes a
miraculous event my family and I encountered
with the Blessed Mother. And I am almost ready
to publish *The Greatest,* which you are looking
at now. I hope to market it and them all as part
of my "How To Live Forever" series targeted to
76 million Baby Boomers and their children and
grandchildren, along with children in difficult

situations who may be in projects and unable to see over the walls. The main theme will be to encourage my generation to write down a piece of their or their family's history which Amazon is currently allowing them to publish as an ebook on Kindle for free. and to preserve their life story *forever* for their great-grandchildren's children.

I tell them, if they are a president or king they won't have to, as it will be done for them, but the rest of us: Nope, etc. There is also a motivational theme, i.e., I use my humble background, poor, SATs, etc., to show their kids and grandkids and any kid who might be in a difficult situation and facing obstacles, how to surmount them to be successful.

In addition, the marketing mantra of my "How to Live Forever" series will allow my five stories to serve as examples of what my fellow Baby Boomers might choose to write of themselves and their families.

Jim Naughton

www.KeyPublishingCompany.com

...AND one last thing.

For my student readers: I will be publishing a book all about my careers, especially my Financial Wholesaling Career to help with your near future decisions: Coming soon!

30 YEARS CARRYING THE BAG

Financial wholesaling During the 80's,90's and 2000s. "Take a ride with a Billion Dollar Wholesaler." Jim Naughton will show you what Financial Wholesaling was like during his era and allow you to peer into the window of a lucrative career.

ABOUT THE DESIGNER

Kip Williams has been my designer and editor for a while now, setting my books up for print and e-book use. He can be reached at his design studio by emailing *mrkipw@gmail.com* for inquiries, rates (reasonable!), and examples of his design and illustration. He strives to be thorough and patient.

www.ingramcontent.com/pod-product-compliance
Lightning Source LLC
LaVergne TN
LVHW022324080426
835508LV00013BA/1307